# ROGER WILLIAMS

# LIVES AND LEGACIES

---

*Larzer Ziff*
## MARK TWAIN

*David S. Reynolds*
## WALT WHITMAN

*Edwin S. Gaustad*
## ROGER WILLIAMS

# ROGER WILLIAMS

---

*Edwin S. Gaustad*

OXFORD
UNIVERSITY PRESS

2005

# OXFORD
UNIVERSITY PRESS

Oxford University Press, Inc., publishes works that further
Oxford University's objective of excellence
in research, scholarship, and education.

Oxford  New York
Auckland  Cape Town  Dar es Salaam  Hong Kong  Karachi
Kuala Lumpur  Madrid  Melbourne  Mexico City  Nairobi
New Delhi  Shanghai  Taipei  Toronto

With offices in
Argentina  Austria  Brazil  Chile  Czech Republic  France  Greece
Guatemala  Hungary  Italy  Japan  Poland  Portugal  Singapore
South Korea  Switzerland  Thailand  Turkey  Ukraine  Vietnam

Copyright © 2005 by Edwin S. Gaustad

Published by Oxford University Press, Inc.
198 Madison Avenue, New York, New York 10016
www.oup.com

Oxford is a registered trademark of Oxford University Press

Library of Congress Cataloging-in-Publication Data
Gaustad, Edwin S. (Edwin Scott)
Roger Williams / Edwin S. Gaustad.
p. cm.—(Lives and legacies)
Includes bibliographical references and index.
ISBN-13: 978-0-19-518369-6
ISBN-10: 0-19-518369-x
1. Williams, Roger, 1604?–1683.  2. Puritans—Rhode Island—Biography.
3. Baptists—Rhode Island—Biography.  4. Separatists—Rhode Island—
Biography.  5. Pioneers—Rhode Island—Biography.  6. Freedom of
religion—Rhode Island—History—17th century.  7. Rhode Island—
History—Colonial period, ca. 1600–1775.  8. Rhode Island—Biography.
9. Rhode Island—Church history—17th century.
I. Title. II. Series.
F82.W7G375  2005  974.5'02'092—dc22  2004025246

1 3 5 7 9 8 6 4 2
Printed in the United States of America
on acid-free paper

To the spiritual heirs of Roger Williams,
to those who agree with him that,
"having bought truth dear, we must not sell it cheap,
not the least grain of it for the whole world."

# ACKNOWLEDGMENTS

I FIRST BECAME INVOLVED WITH OXFORD UNIVERSITY PRESS THROUGH the invitation of Jon Butler of Yale and Oxford vice president Nancy Toff. The working relationship then established has continued for several years, to my very great pleasure. Now, broadening my contacts with the Press, Helen Mules, Senior Production Editor in the Trade Division, has given me the benefit of her expertise and acute guidance in the production of this volume on Roger Williams.

I am grateful to all of these people as well as to the Press in general for the high standards of professionalism carefully maintained. The reading public has reason to be grateful as well.

Santa Fe, NM                                                                    E. S. G.

# Contents

# PREFACE

AT FIRST GLANCE, ROGER WILLIAMS DOES NOT SEEM LIKE A PROMISING subject for a biography. We do not know when he was born, nor exactly when he died. We do not know what he looked like. We cannot visit his home, for it went up in flames long ago. Although he was a preacher, no sermon of his survives. During his lifetime, not a single monument was erected in his honor and, at his death, no carved stone marked his grave. He was—or so it appeared—a forgotten man.

Slowly, however, the memory of the man has begun to be reclaimed. If he was a person well ahead of his times, the times have gradually caught up. Scattered writings about his life, often hurriedly composed, were in the latter half of the nineteenth century gathered together in six volumes; in the twentieth century a seventh volume was added. Recollections of his contemporaries, both friends and foes—he had more of the latter—required more careful examination. Tiny steps that he took in the seventeenth century now look, from the perspective of some three hundred years later, like giant strides.

Williams wrote much about the Native Americans, a great deal about the nature of civil government, but most about the proper relationship between things of the spirit and matters of the sword. We still puzzle over exactly where to draw the line between the authority of the state and the freedom of the soul. We still agonize over the folly of religious persecution, both in America and abroad. And we still worry about the limits of liberty as these relate to calls for responsibility. If any such matters seem urgent in the opening years of the twenty-first century, then Roger Williams needs to be a remembered rather than a forgotten man. His life and his words command our attention.

*One*

---

# THE RESTLESS PURITAN

RELIGIOUS TURBULENCE AND TURMOIL PLAGUED ENGLAND IN THE seventeenth century, as they had in the sixteenth. In the sixteenth century, England, under the prompting of King Henry VIII, had broken with the pope and the Roman Catholic Church. But how "Protestant" this made the newly created Church of England was a much-debated question. Then, in her five-year reign beginning in 1553, Queen Mary I tried unsuccessfully to bring England back into the fold of the Roman church. This created great confusion in both domestic and foreign policy, even as it made suspicions and fears of "Catholic plots" an enduring feature of subsequent English life.

In 1558 Queen Elizabeth I ascended to the throne of England. Her reign, unlike that of her two predecessors, would be a long one: 45 years, ending only with her death in 1603. Historians speak of this period as the "Elizabethan settlement," because many aspects of English life and literature (this was the age of Shakespeare) took on their lasting character then. Religious unrest continued, however, especially among believers who argued that the national Church of England, or Anglican Church, had not become Protestant enough. These fervent Christians thought that England—like Holland and Scotland—should more faithfully follow the theologian John Calvin, then living and writing in Geneva, Switzerland. Many other Protestants had fled during the years that Queen Mary I tried to turn England again toward the Roman Catholic Church. In Geneva many of these refugees sat at the feet of Calvin for their instruction. A generation before Calvin, a German professor and theologian, Martin Luther, launched the Protestant Reformation by rejecting much traditional theology and practice, relying only on the Holy Scriptures. Now Calvin, as a second generation reformer, worked at presenting a more detailed and systematic defense of the Protestant movement.

Elizabeth, however, was not fully persuaded to become a Calvinist. Like her father, King Henry VIII, she steered a middle path between Roman Catholicism on the one hand and an aggressive Calvinism on the other. When she died in 1603, the Tudor dynasty came to an end. To begin a new royal family, James I of Scotland ascended to the English throne in 1603—the first of the Stuart line of England's monarchs. This shift from Tudor kings and queens to Stuart sovereigns hinted at major changes to come. Also, Roger Williams, probably born in this same year, would eventually do more than hint of momentous changes that needed to be made in both politics and religion.[1]

Born in London, Roger Williams grew to manhood during the reign of James I, who ruled until 1625. When James died, Williams would have been about 22 years of age, having begun his college education at Cambridge University, some 50 miles north of London. At Cambridge (one of England's two venerable universities), Williams studied to be a minister in the Church of England. He fell in with other students who shared the passion that this great church should turn away from any lingering traces of Catholicism in order to embrace a consistent and powerful Protestantism. Those who held these strong views came to be called Puritans: persons determined to cleanse their national church of such lingering elements of Catholic practice as bowing at the name of Jesus and making the sign of the cross at baptism. Puritans also believed, unlike Roman Catholics, that clergy should be allowed to marry and should have sufficient learning to preach a sermon at least every Sunday. Bishops should be pastors, not politicians, and the decision to excommunicate a person (that is, eject him or her from the church) should be a spiritual, not a political, decision.

Because James I had grown up in Calvinist Scotland, many Puritans thought he would be sympathetic to their position. He was not. He believed that the Church of England needed to be his close ally in political as well as in spiritual matters. He did agree, however, to one demand of the Puritans: that a new translation of the Bible into English be provided. By virtue of this concession, James managed to associate his name with the most lasting English translation: the King James Version, though, to be sure, he did none of the translating himself. Otherwise, James demanded even stricter conformity to the national church than the English had practiced up to then. This meant that Englishmen and women had to worship in accordance with the prayers and rituals set down in the Book of Common Prayer, the official guide to the church service. Spontaneous prayer and any sort of free-flowing service of worship was not only not allowed, it was illegal. Those who did not conform, identified formally as Nonconformists, fell afoul of England's laws.

To stay in England meant either to conform, at great cost to the Puritans' consciences, or to enter prison, at great cost to their welfare and perhaps even their lives. Some who despaired of ever reforming the bureaucratic Church of England even withdrew from that national body, thereby making themselves targets for arrest and imprisonment. One such group fled to Holland when Roger Williams was still a young boy, and in 1620 emigrated to America aboard the Mayflower. This small fellowship, known in American history as the Pilgrims, settled in Plymouth, Massachusetts, where, years later, their history and that of Roger Williams would intersect.[2]

Meanwhile, back in England, the larger body of Puritans still hoped to change the direction of their national church. They felt that it was indeed their church, their nurturing mother, and they would neither abandon nor forsake it. In the late 1620s, Roger Williams hoped for the reformation of all England and did not want to move toward a separation and exile from his homeland. But if England proved stubborn and unyielding, as James I had been and King Charles I was now proving to be, then a bold and daring step might be required. Some Puritans came up with an ingenious idea: If they could not persuade the great church at home to change its ways, then perhaps they could—in a faraway corner of land—create what they envisioned as the true church of Christ, which could then become the model for the true Church of England. Far from England's intruding and persecuting bishops, protected from the nation's nosy and arresting sheriffs, the Puritans, taking only the New Testament as their pattern and guide, could fashion a pure, nonpolitical, uncorrupted, noncompromised church.

It was bold and daring, so much so as almost to take one's breath away. But gradually, more and more Puritans saw this step as perhaps the only honorable one remaining to them. Not just ministers but lawyers, middle-class farmers, and skilled laborers caught the vision and shared the excitement. Leave England in one sense, but go to England's new lands across the Atlantic, so that they could still be part of their nation and of its church. More than just a part, however—they could be a light, a beacon, an instructor and guide, showing their homeland the path to true Christianity and the meaning of true loyalty. In New England, they would not forsake their nation: They would redeem it.

Late in 1629, Roger Williams married Mary Barnard, the daughter of a clergyman. The young couple, Roger about 26 and Mary 20, had hardly adjusted to their new life together when even greater adjustments were required. For Roger and Mary would soon be part of that large Puritan migration from old England to New. Thousands in the 1630s left farms, families, and fortunes behind to create, in and around Boston, a colony of stability and strength sufficient to leave a permanent stamp upon all of America's later history.[3]

At the end of 1630, Roger and Mary Williams journeyed to the port of Bristol, on England's southwest coast. There they and 20 other passengers boarded the small ship *Lyon* to set out across a treacherous, wintry sea. In less than two months (considered a good crossing in the first half of the seventeenth century) the *Lyon* dropped anchor, on February 5, 1631, off Nantasket, Massachusetts, a few miles south of Boston. The governor of the newly formed Massachusetts Bay Colony expressed his delight at the arrival of the new colonists, and especially of "Mr. Williams, a godly minister," accompanied by his young wife.

The colony had not gotten off to a great start, for food was scarce, housing primitive, and the winter more severe than any known back in England. Death and disease stalked the tiny colony. Yet new arrivals brought with them fresh supplies and new hope. Within a very few years, the pressing question of survival had been settled. The Massachusetts Bay Colony would not only survive but would eventually flourish. John Winthrop, a lawyer and the governor of the Bay Colony, had earlier spoken of his vision of the colony as a "city on a hill." Slowly, the vision began to take on a measure of reality.

Roger Williams's situation seemed quite promising at first. A new colony eager to receive a "godly minister" into its midst, a land of boundless opportunity and promise, a warm welcome from John Winthrop: All this would certainly have worked in Williams's favor. Roger and Mary soon made their way to Boston, the small settlement that would serve as the center for the Massachusetts Bay Colony. There the young couple found welcome, and even the promise of a secure livelihood. Williams was invited to become the resident minister of the newly organized church in Boston—a Puritan church of the type that would later be called "Congregational," a term emphasizing the point that each local congregation ruled itself without the help (or interference) of bishops or church councils.

At this point, however, Williams made a decision as fateful as the one to step aboard the *Lyon* in Bristol. Despite having no other visible means of support, he decided to turn down the job offer because this Puritan church had not clearly, cleanly separated itself from the Church of England. Boston's Puritans still clung to the idea that they could reform the national church from within, that it was not necessary to separate from or reject that nurturing mother. For Williams this seemed an illogical, and perhaps even hypocritical, compromise. How could one profess loyalty to a church while at the same time being dedicated to changing or reforming that church?

So Roger and Mary struck out for Salem, about 15 miles north of Boston, where a church had been organized along more separatist lines, based on thinking more in keeping with Williams's growing conviction that one must leave the Church of England wholly behind. Because ministers were in short supply in Salem, as in Boston, the Salem church took steps to install Williams in a position of leadership. But the Boston authorities, miffed at Williams's refusal to serve their church and disturbed by his separatist "radicalism," advised Salem to hold off hiring Williams as their pastor. (In Congregationalism, each church remained theoretically independent; at the same time, the town of Salem could hardly afford to ignore or alienate the political powers slowly gathering in Boston.) Salem delayed, and Williams was given no official post in the church. But he still talked, still wrote, and still threatened those intent on building that "city on a hill."[4]

If Salem was under the thumb of Boston, perhaps, thought Roger and Mary Williams, they would do better moving about 30 miles south of Boston to the Plymouth Colony. These settlers were unmistakably separatists. Having left the Church of England before they went to Holland, they separated long before they boarded the Mayflower. In Plymouth the restless Roger Williams hoped to find congenial company and a welcoming home. And from late 1631 to the fall of 1633 this almost seemed to be the case. But then, as the Plymouth governor, William Brewster, reported in his valuable history *Of Plimouth Plantation*, Williams "began to fall into some strange opinions, and from opinion to practice." So Williams, rather abruptly, left the church in Plymouth to return to Salem. Though it is not clear just what his "strange opinions" were in Plymouth, his opinions back in Salem soon became all too evident.

Here he could either start an argument or heartily join in arguments already under way. For the next two years in Salem, 1633 to 1635, he in fact did both. One argument in progress concerned the matter of women wearing veils in church, an argument from a question the apostle Paul had put to the church in Corinth: "Is it proper that a woman pray unto God with her head uncovered?" (I Corinthians 11:13).

A Salem pastor, well before Williams's return to that village, had answered that question in the negative: No, it was not fitting for a woman to pray unveiled. Williams agreed, and Boston plunged into the debate. A newly arrived minister, John Cotton, felt that this question related mainly to local customs at the time in Corinth. In Massachusetts, far removed from Paul in both space and time, veiling of women was not required, he announced in Boston, and he journeyed to Salem to make the same point. But of course that hardly settled the matter; the issue only got lost as more disputes came to a boil.[5]

The English flag at the time included a red cross that had been given to the king of England by the pope as a promise of victory in battle. A papal cross in a Puritan flag? To some people in Salem this made no sense, so they proceeded to cut the cross, or a part of it, out of the flag. But defacing and desecrating the national flag? To a good many others, that made no sense; it might even be treason. So the General Court (an executive, legislative, and judicial body) of the Massachusetts Bay Colony rebuked those who acted rashly and "without discretion" in defacing the flag. The rebuke was directed chiefly at John Endicott, the political leader in Salem. Roger Williams was not mentioned in the condemnation, but all Boston knew he was there in Salem, and that wherever controversy erupted he must surely be involved.

On other issues, far more weighty than veils and flags, Williams left no doubt concerning his involvement. Indeed, he led the battle charge. Williams raised serious charges concerning the legal title—a grant or "patent"—of the land given by King Charles I to the Bay Colony. In doing this, Williams questioned the very foundation of the colony's government and legitimacy. Williams was especially troubled by the use of the Christian religion to do a very un-Christian deed: namely, depriving the Indians of their own property without due compensation or negotiation.[6] While in Plymouth, Williams had spent time among the Native Americans and had learned some of their languages and much of their culture. And he realized that they too had rights. English colonization, Williams argued, was "a sin of unjust usurpation upon others' possessions." Christian kings somehow believe that they are invested with right, by virtue of their Christianity, "to take and give away the Lands and Countries of other men." What nonsense, what absurdity!

From the point of view of the General Court, however, what horror, what treachery! Williams, summoned before the court, was asked whether or not he was a loyal subject of King Charles. Did he intend to challenge the authority of the king himself? Did he propose treason, or perhaps revolution? Williams responded, rather mildly for him, that his argument was moral and religious rather than legal or political. And some ministers argued on his behalf that the tract, or statement, he had written on the matter (which no longer survives) was in places ambiguous or "obscure." No charges were levied against him.

But the citizens of Massachusetts were shaken. Was their land not even rightfully their own? Governor John Winthrop responded that land that "lies common, and hath never been replenished or subdued is free to any that possess or improve it." He added that, with respect to the Indians, "if we leave them sufficient for their use, we may lawfully take the rest, there being more than enough for them and us." And pastor John Cotton declared, with some wonderment, "We did not conceive that it is a just title to so vast a continent, to make no other improvement on millions of acres in it, but only to burn it up for pastime." On this question, the clash of cultures, settler and Indian, could not have been more obvious; unhappily, that clash replayed itself in America's history time and again, over the following decades and centuries.

Between Roger Williams and the General Court there had been something of a standoff. Matters might have quietly rested there, if only Williams had left well enough alone. But this he could never quite manage to do. Other matters of Massachusetts policy and procedure continued to trouble him. For example, the Bay Colony required all male inhabitants of 16 years of age or older to swear an oath of allegiance to the colony and the Crown, concluding with the words, "so help me God." But what if the swearer did not believe in God? It made no sense to require an unbeliever to swear by Almighty God, said Williams, though he persuaded few in the seventeenth century and would convince even fewer in later centuries.[7]

Then there was the matter of the duties of the magistrates or civil officers. Did those public officials have a right to enforce such religious duties, as, for example, going to church or keeping the Sabbath day holy? Or, to put it in the language of the day, could the magistrate command obedience to the "first tablet" of the Ten Commandments? These commandments (loving God, avoiding idolatry, not taking the Lord's name in vain, keeping the Sabbath) pertained to the religious order, not the civil order (as the commandments of the "second tablet" did: not stealing, murdering, lying, or committing adultery). But should not the civil and religious orders reinforce and mutually support each other? Almost everyone in the first half of the seventeenth century in Europe and America answered that question with a "yes." Roger Williams answered it with a "no." He was an irritant, surely, but would turn out to be far more than that.[8]

Meanwhile, Williams had been appointed to pastoral duties in the church at Salem. This gave his opinions more status and the flavor of legitimacy. Technically, the Boston authorities could not remove him from a church office in Salem. Politically, however, they had other weapons at their disposal. Salem had applied to the General Court for an additional grant of land. The court thought that, under the circumstances, it made sense to wait on granting that petition until the pressing matter of Roger Williams had been settled. On July 8, 1635, Williams, called before the court once more, was officially warned that his opinions were "erroneous and very dangerous." A warning shot had been fired across his bow. A prudent man would have trimmed his sails and changed his course. Williams, more a man of principle than of prudence, did neither. The moment some concession or compromise seemed possible, he quickly moved on to another position, more extreme, more "dangerous," as the court declared.

Though Williams regarded the court's treatment of himself as unfair, he was even more upset by its riding roughshod over the city and church of Salem. On behalf of the church in Salem, he wrote in late July to the "Elders of the Church at Boston," protesting their lack of Christian charity. Congregations should at least respect, if not love, each other, he argued. The Salem church had earlier written to the Boston church on their side of the argument concerning Williams, but the Boston church's elders had refused even to read that brotherly letter to its own members. If Williams could not find justice with the General Court, he should be able to "find a wisdom greater than theirs" within the church itself. But he and his church had been rebuffed. Was there not a rule of Christ to be considered, as much as a rule of a Massachusetts court? Should the disputing parties not all come together, "for the presence of our souls and bodies together in the presence of the Lord is a gift"? " . . . To punish two or three hundred of our town for the conceived failing of the Church," and to do so before meeting together according to the New Testament rules, was a great evil. Williams concluded, we do not protest any civil matter; rather, "we speak of a spiritual offence against our Lord Jesus."[9]

This appeal to the Boston church, presumably an entity separate from the Boston court, failed to change views in either church or court. In August and September, the parties' respective positions only hardened. Though Roger Williams fell ill, he neither moderated his tone nor shifted his course. For its part, the General Court had been as patient as it felt it could be. But its patience had now run out. Williams, moreover, was losing his following. Many of those who had defended or excused him did so no longer. Even the Salem church was now divided by some of his "dangerous opinions." And so on October 8, 1635, Williams was summoned once more to appear before the court.

The court decided to give Williams a final chance to recant, to take back what he had preached or written. They even sent the learned clergyman Thomas Hooker (later the founder of Connecticut) to spend much of a day and evening with him. But Wil-

liams could not be persuaded that he was wrong. Stubborn, yes—
but not wrong. And so he went back to the court the next morning, October 9, of the same mind and heart. Similarly, the court
could not be persuaded that it was wrong. And so, most solemnly,
the court began: "Whereas Mr. Roger Williams, one of the elders
of the church at Salem, hath broached & divulged diverse new &
dangerous opinions . . . " This "whereas" was followed by several
others that charged him with defying and defaming both the clergy
and the magistrates. From there the court moved to the inevitable
climax: "It is therefore ordered, that the said Mr. Williams shall
depart out of this jurisdiction within six weeks."[10]

Exile, expulsion, rejection. Where would Williams go? With a
wife and a second child born this very October (the first had been
born in Salem two years before), how could he and they survive?
They could not safely return to England, for the Puritans had
themselves found the environment there increasingly hostile. And
if Williams had become too "dangerous" even for the Puritans,
surely King Charles and his persecuting archbishop, William
Laud, would hardly welcome him with open arms. With open
prison gates, more likely. Nor could he hope for refuge in Plymouth Colony, for were it to harbor him as a fugitive, the wrath of
the Massachusetts Bay Colony would certainly turn against it.
What option remained? To escape into the wilderness, beyond
the reach of the General Court, and far beyond the warmth of an
English home.

When the Court granted Williams six weeks to prepare for his
departure from their midst, it stipulated that he was not to go about
drawing others into the black pool of his dangerous opinions.
Williams met that stipulation so far as any public preaching was
concerned. But those who called at his home learned that he had

not changed his mind at all, and so his presence continued to fester. By January, when he showed no sign of leaving and certainly no sign of repenting, the court decided that he must, without further delay, be placed upon a ship then in Boston harbor that was bound for England. From friends, Williams learned of this plan and knew that it promised only greater peril for him. Therefore, he determined that he would not be bound over, like a prisoner, to the ship's captain for a winter voyage to England. He would run.

When the arresting officers arrived at the home of Roger and Mary Williams, "they found that he had been gone three days before; but whither they could not learn." No one could have told them "whither," for Williams himself hardly knew. He would wander for 14 weeks in bitter snow and a "howling wilderness," not knowing what "bed or bread did mean." He had been thrown out by the English; he was taken in by the Indians. At length he came to the headwaters of the Narragansett, about 40 miles southwest of Boston. There he purchased some land from the Indians—with no patent or title from the king. And there he named the tiny settlement "Providence," as he later reported, with a "sense of God's merciful providence to me in my distress."[11]

Near a "sweet spring," as he called it, he started building a shelter. By the spring of 1637 he could send for his wife and two small children to join him. Along with other friends and neighbors from Salem, the community grew to perhaps a dozen families, who began immediately to plant seed for crops that could sustain them by the fall. Meanwhile, friendly Indians offered some foodstuffs, while Williams borrowed money against his house back in Salem in order to purchase hoes and axes. By 1640 nearly 40 families had arrived—enough to begin taking steps toward forming some kind of simple government. That civil government would be care-

first arrives April 1631
returns 1633
**SALEM**

②

**BOSTON**
February 1631

①

③

④

⑤

**PLYMOUTH**
August 1631

**PROVIDENCE**
Spring 1636

Warwick

Portsmouth

Newport

# ROGER WILLIAMS'S MIGRATIONS

This map plots the several moves that Williams made in his first five years in New England: from Boston to Salem to Plymouth; then back to Salem; and finally to Providence in 1636. *Map by Gary Tong* fully separated from the religious order. The founding members, moreover, declared in 1640: "We agree, As formerly hath been the liberties of the Town, so still to hold forth Liberty of Conscience." To some, guaranteeing liberty of conscience may have seemed a small victory; to Roger Williams, this was what his struggle, his exile, his torment were all about.[12]

Making clear what his life was all about occupied Williams in the early months in Providence as he exchanged letters with the Boston pastor John Cotton. Cotton, who had earlier defended Williams, came eventually to believe that Williams really was "dangerous." One could never meet Williams halfway, or agree with him in part. It was all or nothing. Unfortunately, some of those earliest letters have been lost. Enough historical evidence has survived, however, to piece together the fundamental points of disagreement.

Although Cotton and Williams would argue vigorously and at great length against each other, they agreed on many large points. Both were Christians, both were Protestants, both accepted the authority of the Bible, both were graduates of Cambridge University, both were learned clergymen, and both were Puritans— though Williams was clearly the more "restless" thinker of the two. Indeed, Williams recognized this trait when, years later, he spoke of the "restless unsatisfiedness of my soul." Positions vigorously defended today often became mere stopping points on his own "pilgrim's progress." Loyalty to Christ and loyalty to truth seemed always more a quest than a conquest. But he would press on, doggedly, earnestly, and—in the minds of many—perversely.

Remarkably, Williams and Cotton could agree about where their disagreements lay. Four large points divided them. First, in Cotton's words, "that we have not our land by patent from the King, but that the Natives are the true owners of it, and that we ought to repent" for thinking that this land was the king's to give. Williams could not have stated it more fairly himself. This, indeed, did lie at the very heart of his challenge to the political authorities of the Bay Colony. The English were not landowners, they were trespassers. And if the English felt strongly about property rights, so did the Native Americans. For Williams, this was simple truth. But for Cotton this was yet another sign of how cleverly the devil can deceive. "It is no new thing with Satan to transform himself into an Angel of light, and to cheer the soul with false peace, and with flashes of counterfeit consolation." In other words, Cotton argued, Williams's conviction was simply a trick of the devil.[13]

Second, Cotton deplored Williams's claim that an oath sworn in court should be required of only godly persons, of believers. In Cotton's eyes, Williams's problem, or one of them, was that he had an unfortunate tendency to take every idea to its extreme. "You overheated yourself," said Cotton, "in reasoning and disputing against the light" of God's truth. Cotton even regarded an illness that struck Williams in 1635 as God's judgment upon him. But, instead of being chastened, "you chose rather to persist in your way, and to protest against all the Churches and Brethren that stood in your way." The illness that God sent should have humbled you, Cotton argued, but it

John Cotton, a prominent Puritan minister in Boston, proved to be the leading antagonist of Roger Williams on the burning issues of religious liberty and the proper ties between church and state. *New York Public Library, Astor, Lenox and Tilden Foundations: Picture Collection*

only hardened you. Williams, on the other hand, contended that making an unbeliever say "so help me God" forced that person (who did not believe in God) to take "the name of the Lord, thy God, in vain"—which the Third Commandment expressly prohibited.[14]

Third, Cotton continued, Williams would have us renounce and denounce the Church of England in every respect. Here he issued his sharpest challenge to the ecclesiastical authorities. Williams would, Cotton complained, have us "bewail, repent, come out of the false Church's ministry." If Williams spots a sore on a man's leg, he immediately calls for an amputation! He does not know how to move gradually, moderately, peacefully. "We deny," Cotton wrote in a 1636 letter to Williams, "that it is necessary to Church fellowship . . . that the members admitted thereunto should all of them see, expressly bewail all the pollutions which they have been defiled with in the former church fellowship," that is, the Church of England. It is enough that they have condemned some errors, and by removing to the New World are now attempting to create a church more faithful to the New Testament. Even the apostle Paul was willing to work with those still "weak in the faith" and help them to grow more fully in their understanding of what the full gospel requires.[15]

Williams, of course, saw this moderation as fateful compromise and unforgivable hypocrisy. One cannot find, he insisted, a middle ground between Christ and the Antichrist, between loyalty and disloyalty. And yes, sometimes surgery is required if the sore turns into gangrene and threatens the health of the entire body. If the Massachusetts Puritans believed that it was necessary to separate from the rule of bishops, from the demands of the Book of Common Prayer, and from the "prostitution of the ordinances of

Christ," then those same principles should carry them steadily on to all separation of "holy from unholy, penitent from impenitent, godly from ungodly." Well, replied Cotton, you seem determined to "impose a burden on the Church of Christ, which Christ never required at their [the New Testament church's] hands nor yours."

Fourth and finally, Cotton saw nothing but calamity and social anarchy in Williams's bald assertion that the civil magistrate should simply leave religion alone. The magistrate's authority, to hear Williams talk, did not extend to matters of faith, to matters of conscience. True, replied Williams, his authority does not reach into the realm of the sacred. The distinction between the church and the world must always be kept clear; otherwise the "wilderness of the world" will invade the "garden of the church." One must keep a wall or a hedge between the secular and the sacred. This raises the whole matter of religious persecution on the one hand and religious liberty on the other, an issue to which both men give their full attention.[16]

Apart from these four specific points of disagreement between Cotton and Williams, the root of the difficulty lay in the "holier than thou" complex manifest in Williams. Or so Cotton believed. Williams would, he said, be purer than anyone else, his church more "separate" than anyone else's, his allegiance to the New Testament more nearly perfect than that of other faithful Christians. And he would never listen to any reasonings that did not spring out of his own brain. Cotton went on to state, the truth is, Mr. Williams, that the General Court did not banish you: You banished yourself. Williams conceded that in some respects, that may be true, "If Mr. Cotton means my own voluntary withdrawing from those churches resolved to continue" in their evil and polluted practices of worship.

While Cotton claimed that Williams's sentence of exile, his banishment from "common earth and air," was self-inflicted, Williams thought that he could not be more wrong. Williams knew that that wicked argument had been used against Christian martyrs down through the ages. Those in power do not burn or hang or slay you: "[I]t is your schism, heresy, obstinacy" that is responsible. Or, at best, it is the fault of the devil who deceived you, but ultimately your fault for allowing the devil to have his way with you. Besides, Cotton talked as though Williams's civil banishment was a religious punishment, like being exiled from the church. And it is no wonder that he should talk this way, for in Massachusetts the church and the state are the same. As Williams noted, "The Commonweal and Church is yet but one, and he that is banished from the one, must necessarily be banished from the other also." John Cotton has made my point, said Williams, and I rest my case. Cotton simply does not know, does not understand, what the separation of the church from the state is all about.[17]

Cotton's fellow citizens had no difficulty agreeing that the Boston pastor had the best of the argument. After all, he was dealing with a man who kept changing his tune and his direction. He was, exclaimed one contemporary, like a weathervane, moving with every shift of wind, "constant only in his inconstancy." Or, changing the figure, another Bay Colony citizen said that Williams was like a small craft that carried too large and high a sail; it was, therefore, "apt to overset in the stream, and ruin those that are embarked with him." He added, to make matters perfectly clear, that Williams was "a man of a very self-conceited, unquiet, turbulent, and uncharitable spirit." Some even called him "divinely mad." And Cotton himself explained that while the sentence of banishment was "neither done by my counsel or consent . . . I dare not deny the sentence passed to be righteous in the eyes of God."[18]

Williams's enemies did not, however, have the last word. Although Rhode Island prospered slowly, it hung on to become the safest refuge for liberty of conscience. Dissenters of all stripes, persons of all religious persuasions or none, could find sanctuary in Rhode Island. Beside that "sweet spring," Williams sowed the seeds of a sweet liberty. He also came to the defense of Native Americans who had not surrendered their lands and would not, if it pleased God, have to surrender their lives.

## ROGER WILLIAMS AND JOHN WINTHROP
## SEEK AN UNDERSTANDING

*After Roger Williams was banished in 1635, he and John Winthrop exchanged several letters in an effort to explain themselves to each other. Though much of this correspondence has been lost, one letter from Williams to Winthrop, dated October 24, 1636, has survived. In this selection Williams responds to questions that Winthrop had raised.*

Your first query, then, is this: "What have you gained by your new-found practices?"

I confess my gains counted up in man's exchange are loss of friends, esteem, maintenance, etc. But what was "gain" in that respect, I desire to count loss for the excellence of the knowledge of Christ Jesus, my Lord.

To His all glorious name, I know I have gained the honor of one of His poor witnesses, though in sackcloth.

To your beloved selves and others of God's people yet asleep, this witness in the Lord's season at your waking shall be prosperous, and the seed sown shall arise to the greater purity of the Kingdom [of God] and ordinances of the prince of the kings of the earth.

To myself, through His rich grace, my tribulation hath brought some consolation and more evidence of His love . . . .

To your second query: "Is your spirit as even [calm] as it was seven years [ago]?" I will not follow the fashion either in commending or condemning myself. You and I stand at one dreadful tribunal [the Judgment Day]. Yet, what is passed I desire to forget, and to press forward toward the mark, for the prize of the high calling of God in Christ.

As for the evenness of my spirit: Toward the Lord I hope I more long to know and do his holy pleasure only; and to be ready not only to be banished, but to die in New England for the name of the Lord Jesus. . . .

Sir, your fifth [query] is: "From what spirit and to what do you drive?"

Concerning my spirit, as I said before, I could declaim against it, but whether [that spirit] is the spirit of Christ, for whose visible kingdom and ordinances I witness, or the spirit of Antichrist (I John 4) against whom only I do contest, do drive me, let the Father of Spirits be pleased to search. And, worthy Sir, be you also pleased by the word [scripture] to search; and I hope you will find that you can say . . . "I also seek Jesus who was nailed to the gallows." I ask the way to lost Zion; I witness what I believe; I seek patiently (the Lord assisting) in sackcloth; I long for the bright appearance of the Lord Jesus.

# *Two*

---

# WITH THE
# NATIVE AMERICANS

WHILE STILL IN HIS LATE TWENTIES, ROGER WILLIAMS BEGAN A SERIES of close contacts with the American Indians. His two years in the Plymouth Colony, from 1631 to 1633, gave him time to work out some theological problems, to welcome his firstborn (a son) into the world, and to begin a friendship with the Indians. "Friendship" was not the word usually applied to the relations between the English and the Indians, but Williams was the exception here, as in many other respects.

He also took the time and the trouble—as few other English did—to learn the Indians' languages. This skill proved to be of enormous value to him in matters of trade, diplomacy, anthropology, and, most of all, cultural awareness. It was during his Plymouth Colony years that he first began to see the whole colonization enterprise from the Indians' point of view. And from that perspective England's claim (in the person of King Charles I) to ownership of land that the Indians had lived on for hundreds of years struck a false note. When he tried to persuade the Massachusetts Bay Colony to see the "land question" from the point of view of the Indian, he ran into major difficulties. Neither John Winthrop nor John Cotton thought that the Indian point of view had much to recommend it. King Charles spoke for them—and for most other Englishmen up and down the Atlantic seaboard as well.

So when in 1636 Williams began to create a settlement and colony of his own at Providence, he strove to deal fairly with the Native Americans on the crucial issue of land. To obtain land for himself and his family, he first acquired a small acreage from the Indian chief (or sachem), Massasoit, of the Wampanoag tribe. In this and future transactions, Williams insisted that Indian customs and claims be followed, and that everyone agree to fair purchase prices. Even with the best of intentions, however, it was not always possible to avoid misunderstandings, or to find a precise line between competing claims. Williams understood that the power of the sachems was not absolute, that even chiefs had to consult with their subjects. But sometimes kinship had more force than the political structure of a tribe. Persons could even forsake the authority of one sachem for another, so that title disputes became inevitable. Even as Williams struggled to keep the lines of authority and legitimacy clear, so did the sachems themselves struggle to keep the loyalty of their subjects firm.

Then there were the English: They too had claims. When Williams first settled on the land he acquired from Massasoit, he learned from the Plymouth Colony that he had actually settled within the southern limits of their English boundaries. The Plymouth governor "lovingly advised me," Williams wrote, that he should cross to the other side of the Seekonk River, where he would be out of their territorial claim. Williams promptly crossed over that river, putting him out of the Plymouth Colony and farther from the reach of the Bay Colony. This move placed him now, however, in lands that the Narragansett tribe ruled. Negotiating with their sachems Canonicus and Miantonomo, he at last found a more secure site near that "sweet spring" at the head of the Narragansett Bay. Canonicus refused payment, but continued throughout his life (he died in 1647) to accept goods and gifts from Roger Williams. Just prior to his death, the aged chief asked that he be buried with cloth given to him by Williams; this cloth was to be the last of many gifts to Canonicus over the years. He also asked that Williams attend his funeral, for the chief loved him as a son, Williams noted, "to his last gasp." On Williams's part, he added that "when the hearts of my countrymen and friends failed me," then the "infinite wisdom and merits" of Canonicus sustained him. Friendship: If only such warm relationships between the Indian and the English could have been multiplied a hundred times over.[1]

But it could not be and was not. Soon after Williams's family joined him in Providence, tensions arose between the Massachusetts Bay Colony and the Pequot Indians. And though the Bay Colony had exiled Roger Williams, they now found it urgent to call upon his services as negotiator and diplomat, for Williams knew the Indians better than the citizens around Boston did, and he had earned their trust better than they had. Though Governor John Winthrop had voted for Williams's banishment, the two men, remarkably, maintained warm relations until the mid-1640s. Winthrop valued Williams's assistance in many matters, from the raising of goats together on an island in Narragansett Bay to being his eyes and ears regarding the movements and intentions of the Indians.

In July 1636, an English trader was killed off Block Island. Winthrop first suspected the Narragansetts of the deed, but through the intercession of Williams and others he was persuaded that this was not the case. The Pequots were judged responsible. So Massachusetts planned an armed expedition against their strongholds. In late August of that same year, Williams wrote to Winthrop ("Much honored Sir") that "the Pequots hear of your preparations." But they felt secure, because one of their shamans (or "witches") promised to sink the Bay Colony's ships by "diving under water and making holes" in them below the waterline. The Pequots also dreamed of capturing a great many guns from those moving against them, "but I hope their dreams through the mercy of [the] Lord shall vanish."[2]

Their dreams did not vanish, but their kingdom did. First, through labored negotiations Roger Williams persuaded the Narragansetts not only to sever all ties with the Pequots but even to join with soldiers from the Bay Colony in attacking them. When the General Court in Boston hurriedly wrote Williams to do his best to break the alliance between the Narragansetts and the Pequots, Williams, scarcely taking time to bid his wife good-bye, jumped in a "poor canoe" to row all by himself through "a stormy wind 30 miles in great seas, every minute in hazard of life" to the home of Canonicus. There, for three days and nights, he bargained with the Narragansetts. He also met with, and even lodged with, ambassadors from the Pequots, who "reeked with the blood of my countrymen, murdered and massacred by them on [the] Connecticut River." Williams added, "I could not but nightly look for their bloody knives at my own throat also." Though he succeeded in making peace with the Narragansetts, he failed to do so with the Pequots.[3]

Blood had been shed on both sides, and more would soon pour forth. A combined force of Connecticut militia, Mohegans, and Narragansetts attacked the Pequot fort at Mystic, Connecticut, on May 26, 1637. After only an hour of fierce fighting, several hundred Pequots, including women and children, had lost their lives. But the English were not through. When reinforcements arrived from Massachusetts, the fleeing Pequots were pursued—to be killed or enslaved and sold to buyers in the West Indies. By the time the Pequot War formally ended in September 1638, the tribe as a political entity was finished. For almost half a century after this war, a pervasive if uneasy peace existed between the Indians and the English in New England. In all this, the services of Roger Williams had been so valuable that he even heard rumors that some in Massachusetts considered "whether or no I had not merited not only to be recalled from banishment, but also to be honored with some remark of favor." But if Williams had some friends in Massachusetts, he had enemies in greater abundance. The banishment remained; the honor was never bestowed.[4]

Perhaps as early as 1637, Williams undertook the role of a trader with the Indians. Near the present site of Wickford, Rhode Island (about 20 miles south of Providence), Williams established a trading post that, with major interruptions, he endeavored to maintain until near the end of his life. The site, laid out for him by his good friend Canonicus, was on a cove of the Narragansett Bay. This site gave Williams a great advantage for shipping goods to or receiving them from abroad. Williams traded cloth, seed, cooking utensils, and simple tools, but strongly resisted any trading in guns or munitions. This latter trade would have made more money for Williams, but it would have been a cruelty to his Indian clients. For the same reason, he declined to trade in strong liquors, except in small amounts to be used as medication during serious illnesses. The Indians bartered with furs, skins, pottery, and baskets for whatever Williams had that they wanted. Over the years, Williams expanded his trade to include the English to the north and the Dutch to the south (in New York, then called New Amsterdam). But throughout, in his capacity as an honest trader, Roger Williams concerned himself chiefly with the Indians.

In 1643, Williams found it necessary to leave his still small and vulnerable colony for a long voyage to London. The primary reason for his trip was to secure firmer legal standing for Rhode Island. At the time of Williams's trip, the colony had no charter; moreover, Massachusetts from the north, Connecticut from the east, and the Dutch from the south looked upon Rhode Island's lands as ripe for picking, or plucking, or annexing. Without some recognition from the government in England, Aquidneck Island was exposed on all sides to stronger or hungrier forces.

But a secondary purpose guided Williams as well. He had, since the mid-1630s, been doing a good bit of writing, but Rhode Island had no presses capable of publishing a book. Boston did have such presses, but the city fathers were in no way disposed to print anything written by their banished, wayward brother. If Williams was to be published, therefore, his best opportunity awaited him in London. And so several treatises from his pen at last reached a wider public in 1643–44.

His first and most popular book concerned the Indians. Published in 1643, it was called *A Key into the Language of America.* The use of the word "language" suggests that it might be a dictionary, and that, in part, is the case. But it is much more than that. As its title page indicates, it is also an early and valuable example of cultural anthropology, or in Williams's words, *"with brief Observations of the Customs, Manners, and Worships . . . in Peace and War, in Life and Death."* This would seem to be quite enough, but Williams had still more to offer. He wanted also to include *"Spiritual Observations, General and Particular, by the Author."* These "observations," usually given in poetic form, were designed mainly to instruct the English, who had a tendency to think of themselves and their culture as vastly superior to anything the Indians might know or do. This attitude, said Williams, was folly, noting that his book would attempt to expose that unwarranted pride.[5]

The *Key* made a great hit in London, for the English were burning with curiosity to know more about the North American "savages." Most of them had never seen an American Indian, and none of them had lived among them as Williams had. In addition, the book was written with a simplicity of style that quickly engaged the reader. Beyond that, it was written with

A KEY into the
# LANGUAGE
*OF*
# AMERICA:
*OR,*
An help to the *Language* of the *Natives* in that part of AMERICA, called *NEW-ENGLAND.*

Together, with briefe *Observations* of the Customes, Manners and Worships, &c. of the aforesaid *Natives*, in Peace and Warre, in Life and Death.

On all which are added Spirituall *Observations,* Generall and Particular by the *Authour,* of chiefe and speciall use (upon all occasions) to all the *English* Inhabiting those parts; yet pleasant and profitable to the view of all men:

*BY* ROGER WILLIAMS *of Providence in New-England.*

*LONDON,*
Printed by *Gregory Dexter,* 1643.

Roger Williams's first and most popular book, both in England and America, this *Key* continues to provide valuable insights into the culture of the early Narraganset Indians. *Courtesy of the Rhode Island Historical Society* "magnanimity, compassion, personal freedom and freshness," as an expert in American literature declared many decades ago.[6] The logical progression of the book was from one's first encounter with an Indian ("of Salutations") to one's final resting place ("of Death and Burial"). Along the way, Williams provided Indian vocabulary, with aids to pronunciation, together with English translations— something like a modern phrasebook for someone traveling in a foreign country.

Williams began his chapter on greetings with the observation that the Indians, like the English, are not all of one character or temperament: Some are "rude and clownish," others are "sober and grave." Some will be the first to greet a stranger politely, while others will wait until they have been initially acknowledged. There is nothing too surprising about any of this. And again, like the English, the Indians "are exceedingly delighted with being greeted in their own language." With Williams's *Key*, this became possible, particularly among the Narragansetts, whose dialect makes up most of the vocabulary in the book. For example, if one wanted to ask an Indian, "How are you?" one would say, "Askuttaaquompsin?" And the Narragansett might well reply, "Asnpaumpmaûntam," that is, "I am very well." Of course, it might take a little practice to get this down just right—as would Spanish, German, French, or Japanese.[7]

On the matter of personal names, Williams pointed out that these were largely for private rather than public use. Most of the time, one would address an Indian as "you" or "he" or "she." But when a sachem died, his personal name died with him. If another Indian happened to have the same personal name, he no longer used it, saying, "I have forgotten my name." The fact that the Indians had many expressions for hospitality, such as "Come hither, friend," or "Sit by the fire," indicates what Williams found to be true over and over: "They are remarkably free and courteous." They have hearts "sensible of kindnesses," leading Williams to conclude that "there is a savor of civility and courtesy even among these wild Americans, both amongst themselves and towards strangers." Indeed, the English ("sons of God") could learn from them, as the author notes here in poetic form.

> If Nature's sons both wild and tame,
> Humane and courteous be;
> How ill becomes it sons of God
> To want [lack] humanity?[8]

Williams's close observations are fully evident in a chapter entitled "Of Eating and Entertainment." Roasted corn or cornmeal was a staple of the Indian diet, in their own villages as well as when they were on the road. Williams once traveled with some two hundred Indians for one hundred miles or more, and all they carried in the way of food was their parched meal in a backpack or in a leather girdle around their middle. This was sufficient to keep a man going for three or four days. "With a spoonful of this meal and a spoonful of water from the brook, have I made many a good dinner and supper," Williams reported. The English, however, preferred to have their meal with milk or butter, "which are mercies beyond the native's plain water."[9]

For relief and refreshment, most Indians used tobacco. This plant was helpful in cases of toothache, "which is the only pain that will force their stout hearts to cry." But on long journeys they also resorted to tobacco "to revive and refresh them, they drinking nothing but water." If a stranger happened upon them while they ate, they would invite him in, "though but little enough prepared for themselves." And if they happened to have meat or fish, that too was freely shared. "It is a strange truth," Williams concluded, "that a man shall generally find more free entertainment and refreshing amongst these barbarians, than amongst thousands that call themselves Christians." Or, more poetically:

Sometimes God gives them fish or flesh,
Yet they're content without;
And what comes in, they part to friends
And strangers round about.[10]

The Indians originally had no drums of their own, but they managed to make some in imitation of the English. And they had no horns, but bought a few from the Dutch. Their normal method of raising an alarm was simply to holler, and whoever heard this clamor passed it on along the line of small villages—sometimes as many as one hundred in a distance of only 20 miles. The Indians slept on straw lots of it—with no bedclothes. The fire served as their only cover: If the night was very cold, one "must be content to turn often to the fire." Whoever woke up first in the morning had the duty to "repair the fire." Here again, the behavior of the Indians came off better than that of the Europeans.

I have known them leave their house and mat
To lodge a friend or stranger,
When Jews and Christians oft have sent
Christ Jesus to the manger.[11]

In their villages, the Indians took the ties of kinship very seriously. If one of their number was slain, the next of kin had to seek revenge at all costs. Also, if the parents of young children died or were slain, the village as a whole immediately adopted the orphans as their own. And no beggars were to be found among them. Children were indulged—too much so, in Williams's opinion—with the result that most of them were "saucy, bold, and undutiful." If a village had been spared from sickness or plague (such as the European-imported smallpox), then commonly the number of children was large, for the natives "increase mightily."[12]

The Indians frequently took more than one wife, Williams noted, and chiefly for two reasons. First, a "desire for riches," because each wife generally brought some possessions from her family, called a dowry, with her and because her labor in the fields increased the harvest for the husband, who only fished and hunted. Second, when a wife was pregnant, and for as long as a year after birth (as long as the child was "at the breast"), the wife kept apart from the husband. A second, third, or fourth wife was, therefore, a great convenience, though the Narragansetts, Williams reported, generally took but one wife. Most Indians did not frown on sex before marriage, but adultery—both male and female—after marriage was severely punished. If a woman was adulterous, the husband took his revenge not upon her but upon the offending male: "before many witnesses, by many blows and wounds, and if it be to death, yet the guilty resists not, nor is his death revenged."[13]

For the most part, Indian women bore their young without pain or complaint. Williams explained this first in terms of their hardy constitutions and second because of their continuous, heavy physical labors. They cultivated the fields, brought in the harvest, dug for clams and other shellfish, and beat "all their corn in mortars." "Most of them count it a shame for a woman in travail to make complaint." Indeed, Williams reported, "I have often known in one quarter of an hour a woman merry in the house, and delivered, and merry again; and within two days abroad, and after four or five days at work." Indians uniformly honored the marriage bed, and had no understanding of a religious demand for priests to remain unmarried.[14]

Describing the physical bodies of the Indians, Williams made the point that all humankind was one. "Nature knows no difference," he wrote, "between Europeans and Americans [i.e., Indians] in blood, birth, bodies, etc., God having of one blood made mankind." This, of course, had implications for the relationships that should exist between peoples of different cultures or races, implications that found this poetic expression:

> Boast not proud English, of thy birth and blood,
> Thy brother Indian is by birth as Good.
> Of one blood God made him, and thee, and all,
> As wise, as fair, as strong, as personal
>> [i.e., a person with all the rights and dignity
>> of a full human being].[15]

The natives lived in close touch with nature, day by day, month by month. They observed the seasons and had names for summer, fall, winter, and spring. They kept time, not as the English did, but by observing the sun and moon.

> They have no help of clock or watch,
> And Sun they overprize.
> Having these artificial helps, the Sun
> We unthankfully despise.[16]

From childhood, the Indians learned the woods and the trails, the resting and hiding places. The English got lost in the vast wilderness, but rarely, Williams noted, did the Indians. "I have often been guided twenty, thirty, sometimes forty miles through the woods, a straight course," without any path or trail in sight. They also learned at an early age to run, and all did so. But some especially excellent runners could cover from 80 to 100 miles "in a summer's day." Within two days, the runner would be ready to retrace his steps. Despite all this, the Indians loved to ride horses, but they owned very few because they could not afford the "English prices."[17]

And so Williams wrote of the Indian view of the stars, of the winds and storms, of the earth and its fruits. He said they fed on geese, turkeys, cranes, and other fowl, which tended to be bountiful in all the bays, swamps, and inlets along the Atlantic shore. The birds were so abundant that special steps had to be taken to keep them out of the fields. Instead of scarecrows, the Indians lodged their older children in small shelters around the corn. As day broke, the children knew their duty: Scare the birds all away. Sometimes they even domesticated hawks, which were by nature well equipped to keep the other birds far from the fields. They also gathered nuts and berries, and if the corn crop failed, they gathered acorns that, after drying and boiling, became edible. Williams was especially ecstatic about the strawberries, reporting that God could have, but never did, make a better berry. The English, Williams reluctantly admits, put the strawberries and grapes to even better use by making fine wines, "as I have often tasted." But in fishing and hunting, the Indians excelled in their marksmanship and their nets.[18]

Indians were more often naked than clothed, except for small aprons. Yet, said Williams, their behavior is modest and restrained. In fact, he added, "I could never discern that excess of scandalous sins amongst them, which Europe aboundeth with. Drunkenness and gluttony—generally they know not what sins they be."

Observing the habits and manners of English traders who moved among them, the Indians had reason to feel some superiority of their own. As Williams wrote on their behalf:

We wear no clothes, have many gods,
And yet our sins are less;
You are barbarians, pagans wild,
Your land's the wilderness.[19]

The Indians used seashells and beads for money, since they had no coins of their own. Sometimes, of course, they simply bartered, trading their furs or baskets for hoes or axes. They hung the strings of beads, or wampum, around their necks or wrists and "upon the necks and wrists of their wives and children." For trading, some Indian specialists concentrated only on the making of bows or arrows or dishes, the latter being an occupation chiefly of women. Indians who lived near the seashore collected shells in the summer, then made money out of the shells during the winter. In one of his few complaints against the Indians, Williams noted that they were not prompt about paying their debts. Sometimes it was necessary to follow them "to their several abodes, towns, and houses, as I myself have been forced to do." Then Williams might have been met with the excuse that they had been ill and had been forced to pay the medicine man who came to heal them. Or they complained, as the English also did, that the price of goods changed from year to year, according to market demands that they hardly understood and were in no mood to accept as an explanation. Whoever deals with them, said Williams, must have wisdom, patience, and honesty, for the Indians were ever ready to say, "You deceived me." Furthermore, "They are marvelously subtle in their bargains to save a penny," and will run 20 miles or more to save a sixpence.[20]

Given the training of Roger Williams at Cambridge University, as well as his intense involvement in matters religious, one would certainly expect him to observe with the keenest interest the religion of his neighboring Indians. And so he did. He counted the many names they had for God or the gods (37 in all), and noted how they saw divine power in any excellence observed around them. When Indians talked among themselves, Williams commented, they even spoke of such things as English ships, great buildings, iron plows, and books as indications of the divine spirit. "A strong conviction natural in the soul of man," Williams wrote, was "that God is—filling all things, and places, and that all excellencies dwell in God, and proceed from him."[21]

The Indians held private ceremonies, or feasts, in times of sickness, drought, war, and famine throughout the year. But their great public feast came chiefly in the late fall, after all the harvest was in, and "a calm of peace, health, plenty, [and] prosperity" settled upon them. Then, as among the Christians at Christmas, there was much joy and revelry and feasting. On other occasions, neighbors would give a feast and perhaps donate money on behalf of a person who was then obliged to call out loudly to the gods for "the health and prosperity of the party that gave it." Williams testified that he had often gathered with 20, 50, 100, or even "near a thousand persons at one of these Feasts." Perhaps because he was looking for it so intently, Williams even found a kind of religious freedom among the natives. "They have a modest religious persuasion not to disturb any man, either themselves, English, Dutch, or any in their conscience and worship."[22]

Finally, Williams concludes his *Key* with attention to sickness, death, and burial among the Native Americans. In sickness, Williams was himself often called upon to render what assistance or comfort he could, "beyond my power," because they had few medicines at hand. But if a plague such as smallpox struck a village, all recognized that any cure was beyond their power or that of the English. Then the only option was to flee. "I have often seen a poor house left alone in the woods, all being fled, the living not able to bury the dead, so terrible is the apprehension of an infectious disease." For less serious illnesses, the Indians often resorted to a kind of sauna or "sweat lodge" that had been "exceedingly heated with a store of wood, laid upon a heap of stones in the middle." After a time, the fire was removed, but the stones stayed hot. At that point, ten or twelve "enter at once, stark naked . . . here they do sit around these hot stones an hour or more, taking tobacco, discoursing, and sweating together." After that hour, "I have seen them run (summer and winter) into the brooks to cool them, without the least hurt."[23]

Death was, for the natives as for all "natural men," the "King of Terrors." At the grave site, lamentations and tears were common. Often, bows and arrows or money would be placed in the grave to assist the dead in their transition to a better afterlife. "Sometimes a fair coat of skin [will be] hung upon the next tree to the grave, which none will touch, but [leave] it there to rot with the dead."[24]

Williams even observed his aged friend Canonicus burn his own house and all within it when his son died, "as a kind of humble [appeasement] to the gods, who (as they believe) had taken his son from him." Williams concluded his work with a noble benediction, praying to the most high "and only wise God" and thanking him for the "wonderful supportment" that enabled Williams to study and converse with the Indians and "to frame this poor Key." He dared to hope and pray that his book would somehow open "doors of mercy to us and them," the first Americans.[25]

In his introduction to the *Key,* Williams acknowledged that he had not addressed in it one class of questions: "What Indians have been converted? What have the English done in those parts? What hopes of the Indians receiving the knowledge of Christ?" Admitting that this was "the great inquiry" back in England, Williams indicated that he would soon "present you with a brief additional discourse concerning this Great Point." This tract, long lost from the collection of Williams's writing but finally rediscovered some two hundred years after his death, is entitled *Christenings Make Not Christians.*

A good part of its message is contained in the title: A mere outward religious ritual does not alter the condition of one's heart. A christening or a baptism, to be sure, can be a powerful symbol, but it can also be an empty one if a life is not changed or set upon a new path. With regard to the Indians, who were generally unable to read the Bible and could not understand a creed or catechism without extensive tutoring, a so-called conversion might prove to be only an empty gesture. This was certainly true when conversion came at the point of a sword, as had so often been the case in earlier centuries. Williams denounced these "monstrous and most inhumane conversions" as a violation of the Indians' spiritual integrity. What could be worse than this cruel practice of making Christians of thousands, "yea, tens of thousands by wiles and subtle devices, sometimes by force compelling them to submit to that which they understood not?" Williams would have none of it.[26]

Therefore, though he knew the Indians better than most, though they trusted him more than they did most Englishmen, Williams decided that he would not seek to convert them. In this refusal he knew he would be misunderstood, and so he was. But his position was firm. "Woe be to me," he wrote, "if I call light darkness or darkness light. . . . Woe be to me if I call that conversion unto God, which is indeed subversion of the souls of millions in Christendom, from one false worship to another." Here Williams had in mind not only what was happening to native populations all over the world but the unhappy example of a West Germanic king in the Middle Ages who drove his army through a river, thereby "baptizing" them and making "Christians" of them all—in an instant. This charade made a mockery of everything that religion in general, or Christianity in particular, stood for.[27]

Williams knew that forced conversion was no conversion at all. A required conformity or "some external submission" to a christening or a baptism or the observance of Sunday or formal prayers was no conversion at all. Worse, it possibly worked as a kind of inoculation or prevention against sincere religion. When a dominant culture or a powerful nation imposed its religion upon a weak and vulnerable people, it did not further the cause of Christianity; rather, it undermined it. The Native Americans, Williams believed, deserved better than religious persecution disguised as religious evangelism. What was to be done? Wait upon God, Williams replied. In accordance with God's own timetable, which is beyond our understanding, the time for the conversion of the Native Americans will finally arrive.[28]

In the *Key*, Williams recounted a conversation with his close Indian friend, Canonicus. Williams learned that Canonicus, like all New England Indians, worried about the growing number of English arriving from abroad. And like many, he wondered if the English were dealing with the Indians—and himself—fairly. "In a solemn oration to myself, in a solemn assembly," Williams noted, Canonicus announced that he had never permitted "any wrong to be offered to the English since they landed, nor never will." Then, this "wise and peaceable prince," as Williams called him, added: "If the Englishman speak true, if he means truly, then shall I go to my grave in peace and hope that the English and my posterity shall live in love and peace together." Tragically, it was not to be.[29]

When Canonicus and Williams conversed in the 1630s, the flow of English emigration to New England was still comparatively limited, and the occupation of lands in the Northeast was still relatively restricted. A half-century later, this was no longer the case. By then Massachusetts's inhabitants had pushed westward into the interior, settling on both sides of the Connecticut River. Some had moved northeast into what would become New Hampshire, others southwest into what would become Connecticut. Immigrants continued to pour in from abroad, and the English, no less than the Indians, managed to "increase mightily." More farms went into cultivation and more towns sprang from the soil. By the 1670s, more and more Indians concluded that the very ground was disappearing from under them. Misunderstandings only multiplied, as population pressures intensified. In their growing frustration, all the Native Americans needed was a leader.[30]

That leader, Metacomet (known as "King Philip" to the English), was the son of Massasoit, the sachem of the Wampanoags around Plymouth. These were the people who had first sold land to Roger Williams, land that he later abandoned because it was within the borders of the Plymouth Colony. That was in 1636. Now, in the 1670s, rumors flew of Indian plots involving an armed attack against the English. When Metacomet worried and antagonized the English, Williams was once more called upon to take up his familiar role as diplomat and negotiator. At one point, he even gave himself up to the Wampanoags as a hostage to assure them that the Plymouth Colony would return their leader safely. Meta-comet did return to his home, but only after surrendering some 70 guns in his possession. (In a mere half-century, guns had largely replaced bows and arrows among the Indians.) And Roger Williams was also allowed to return to his home safely.

But tensions and resentments continued to smoulder and build, especially in the Plymouth Colony. By 1675, rumors ran furiously once again: that Metacomet was rearming himself, that some major conflict was imminent. An Indian informer carried this word to the authorities at Plymouth; when the Wampanoags heard of this betrayal, they killed the messenger. Then, when Plymouth heard of that murder, they arrested three men suspected of the crime and condemned them to death. On June 13, Williams wrote to John Winthrop, Jr. (governor of Connecticut and son of Williams's now-deceased old friend from Massachusetts Bay): "Sir, it is true that Philip (fearing apprehension) stood upon his guard with armed barbarians." The Plymouth Court decided that it did not have sufficient evidence to put the three men to death, and so "let matters sleep." Williams hoped that at this point quiet would settle on the country.[31]

He hoped in vain. For now, to complicate matters enormously, the Wampanoags moved to forge an alliance with the much larger, much stronger Narragansetts—the old friends and trading partners of Roger Williams. The Massachusetts colony, upon hearing of this possibility, grew greatly alarmed. Representatives of the governor hurried to Providence to enlist Williams in a hastily arranged parley to keep the Narragansetts at peace. Told of this mounting concern, the Narragansetts informed Williams and the others that they "held no agreement with Philip in this rising against the English." They even promised that if Metacomet or any of his men "fled to them, yet they would not receive them, but deliver them up unto the English." Had Williams succeeded again? Now in his seventies, he concluded a second letter, dated June 25, 1675, to John Winthrop, Jr., with these poignant words: "Sir, my old bones and eyes are weary with travel and writing to [governors] of Massachusetts and Rhode Island and now to yourselves."[32]

But Williams had not succeeded. What historians now speak of as King Philip's War broke out only a few days later—with the Narragansetts and others in league with the Wampanoags. The Indian attack was widespread, ferocious, and successful—beyond anyone's imagination—and it was almost beyond the ability of the English to keep from being pushed back into the sea. Virtually all the frontier towns and villages were burned to the ground, with their inhabitants slain or scattered. Massachusetts pressed all able-bodied men from 16 to 60 into military service, promising bonuses of land in addition to their regular pay. Connecticut passed a law prohibiting any potential fighting man from leaving the colony. Even Roger Williams concluded that it was necessary for him to accept duty in the Rhode Island militia.

By December of 1675, Williams had lost all hope of being able to pour oil on very troubled waters. Negotiation had failed, diplomacy was done. To John Winthrop, Jr., he wrote on December 18 that "I presume you are satisfied in the necessity of these present hostilities, and trust that it is not possible at present to keep peace with these barbarous men of blood." They must, he felt, be dealt with as one deals with the wolves that attack a flock of sheep. In the winter, Williams found it necessary to send his own wife to the island of Aquidneck, where other Rhode Islanders had fled and where wounded soldiers were sent for convalescence. In late March, the native warriors attacked Providence, sending most of the buildings and houses up in flames, including Roger Williams's own home. The bonds forged decades earlier between Williams and Canonicus were forever broken.[33]

In the number of lives lost and property ruined, King Philip's War was, in proportion to the population at that time, America's deadliest and costliest war. Massachusetts alone had casualties in the many hundreds, as did the Indians. Fifty-two of New England's 90 towns had suffered from attack; many were totally destroyed. "King Philip" himself was captured and killed on August 12, 1676, effectively bringing the bitter hostilities to an end. Now it was time to reestablish lines of commerce and replant the devastated fields. It was also time to rebuild towns and homes. Trust between the English and the Indians, however, could not be rebuilt.

Williams had expended himself and his property on behalf of the English with such sacrifice that Massachusetts was moved on March 31, 1676, to temporarily suspend his banishment as long as he refrained from "venting any of his different opinions." Those sacrifices had reduced him to poverty. He even had to beg the Massachusetts governor for writing paper, because he often found it necessary to write on "public business" and was "now near destitute." Whether Massachusetts ever responded to this sad request is not known.[34]

## The Key to Unlock Many Doors

*In his popular and still useful* A Key into the Language of America *(1643), Roger Williams introduced his treatise in this fashion (from* The Complete Writings of Roger Williams):

To my dear and well beloved friends and countrymen, in old and new England:

I present you with a Key. I have not heard of the like, yet framed, since it pleased God to bring that mighty continent of America to light. Others of my countrymen have often, and excellently, and lately, written of the country—and none that I know of beyond the goodness and worth of it.

This key respects the native language of [that country], and happily may unlock some rarities concerning the Natives themselves, not yet discovered.

I drew the materials in a rude lump at sea, as a private help to my own memory, that I might not by my present absence lightly lose what I had so dearly bought in some few years hardships and burdens among the barbarians. Yet, being reminded by some, what pity it [would be] to bury those materials in my grave at land or sea; and [besides] remembering how often I have been [asked] by worthy friends of all sorts to afford them some helps this way, I resolved (by the assistance of the most High) to cast those materials into this Key, pleasant and profitable for all, but especially for my friends residing in those parts.

A little Key may open a box, where lies a bunch of Keys.

With this [key] I have entered into the secrets of those countries, wherever the English dwell, about two hundred miles between the French and the Dutch plantations. For want of this [key], I know what gross mistakes myself and others have run into.

There is a mixture of this language north and south, from the place of my abode, about six hundred miles; yet, within the two hundred miles aforementioned, their dialects do exceedingly differ. Yet not so [much] within that compass a man may, by this help, converse with thousands of Natives all over the country. And by such converse, it may please the Father of Mercies to spread civility and—in His most holy season—Christianity. For one candle will light ten thousand, and it may please God to bless a little leaven to season the mighty lump of those people and territories.

It is expected that having had so much converse with these Natives, I should write some little of them.

Concerning them, a little to gratify expectation, I shall touch upon four heads:

first, by what names they are distinguished;
second, their origin and descent;
third, their religion, manners, customs, &c.;
fourth, that great point of their conversion.

*Three*

# FOUNDER OF
# RHODE ISLAND

During his five years in the Massachusetts and Plymouth colonies, Roger Williams was always the outsider: complaining about this or that practice, agitating for this or that reform. But as of the middle of 1636, he was the insider. Now he could not protest against the authorities, for suddenly he had become the authority. He had a town and a colony to run, and how did one do that, anyway?

Williams had been banished into a wilderness. And a wilderness, by definition, has no trails or paths. In addition, no paths opened up before him in the matters of government, for which he was now responsible. He could not keep moving; he had a family to support; he had several causes to serve; somehow, he had to succeed. Some of the friends and neighbors from Salem who decided to join him in Providence could come and go as they pleased. Roger Williams could not—he had to make things work. And he knew it would not be easy. A few years later he wrote of this time as one filled only with "miseries, poverties, necessities, wants, debts, hardships of sea and land." That was not much of a foundation on which to build either a colony or a town.[1]

So where should he start, and how should he begin? In the summer of 1636, he wrote to John Winthrop for advice, because Winthrop had by then been governing a colony for about six years. "I shall humbly crave your help," Williams freely acknowledged. For the town of Providence had no legal authorization from the king, or anyone else back in England. It certainly had no authorization from the Massachusetts Bay Colony, and at this point it lacked even a church structure that might have granted some stability and direction. In such a sea of uncertainty, Williams could only improvise. This, so far, is what we have done, he told Winthrop: "The masters of families have ordinarily met once a fortnight [every two weeks] and consulted about our common peace, watch, and planting." That is, decisions would be arrived at not by dictatorial authority but by mutual consent. All would have some obligation to join in the watch: that is, to be on guard against an Indian attack (especially from the Pequots) and to sound an alarm in the case of any other emergency, such as fire. Planting, of course, was most urgent, for the community of 30 or so persons could look only to itself for sowing seed and reaping a harvest.[2]

The program was modest enough: Let us work together as sensibly as we can, but let us work. Williams encouraged each head of a household to sign a covenant, or agreement, that would bind them to come together "with free and joint consent" and "to promise each unto other" that whatever the majority decided to do, all would obey. As new arrivals came, they, too, would be obliged to sign this agreement. One person would be named the town officer, whose duty it would be to call meetings and gather votes on the issues that came before them. Roger Williams was one of the first to serve in that capacity. The few surviving notes from the first years show him writing "in the name of the King and Parliament of England" in an effort to give some force or standing to these tentative steps toward self-government.[3]

Having acquired title to the land from the Narragansett Indian chiefs, in 1636 Williams proceeded to divide parcels of land among the first settlers. Each parcel was a narrow strip that began down by the spring, and then moved up the steep hill to its top. Williams's parcel was the same size as everyone else's. Few written records were kept of these earliest transactions, which only added to Williams's many difficulties in trying desperately to settle endless disputes about land. The English thirst for land, Williams observed, was very strong, as though they had just come from a "long and starving passage" at sea. They could not wait to set their feet on firm soil that they could call their own. Land, Williams concluded, was one of the "gods of New England." Having seen the greed of so many, Williams—who certainly had the strongest claim of any to large parcels of land—carefully refrained from bowing down to that New England god. He never amassed land for himself, never feathered his own nest. As he wrote, "I desire not to sleep in security and dream of a nest which no hand can reach." From time to time, his wife no doubt would have wished for a little more thought about that safe and warm nest.[4]

As Williams labored for some semblance of stable town government, he also recognized the necessity for stability in the church's organization. He had criticized the Puritan churches and described what seemed to him to be a better way for the church: complete separation from the Church of England and full separation of civil power from spiritual activity. For those moving into his colony, Williams had ordered that "no man should be molested for his conscience."[5]

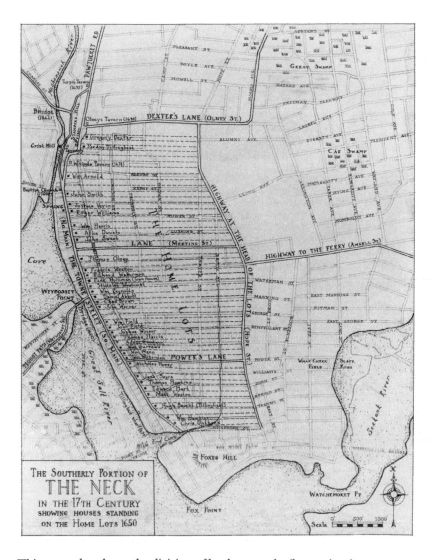

THE SOUTHERLY PORTION OF
# THE NECK
IN THE 17TH CENTURY
SHOWING HOUSES STANDING
ON THE HOME LOTS 1650

This town plan shows the division of land among the first settlers in Providence. The long and narrow lots ran from the river and Town Street up the steep hill behind the home sites. All grants of land, including Roger Williams's, were of equal size. *Courtesy of the Rhode Island Historical Society*

But while this was a most valuable directive, it did not by itself provide any positive option of what to do with one's conscience as far as sacred worship was concerned. It was time for the town of Providence, only two years in the making, to have a church.

But what sort of church? Not the Church of England, of course, nor Puritan. What then? Attracted to the idea of separation and to those who in England had been persecuted for their separatism, Williams was further attracted to those who argued that one should come into a church only through her or his voluntary consent. Infants should not be baptized into a church that they had not chosen. Nor should people automatically be counted as members of a national or official church just because they lived in a certain territory or within the bounds of a specified parish. Baptism should be administered not to some bawling babe in arms as the Puritans did, but only to adult believers who had, voluntarily, offered a confession of their personal faith. In the first half of the seventeenth century, the English Baptists came closest to the position that Roger Williams had staked out. And in fact, his enemies in Massachusetts kept pushing him into the Baptist camp as they charged him with various departures from orthodoxy, or traditional Christian doctrine, associated with the name (or with the name "Anabaptist," meaning rebaptizer, that Massachusetts regularly preferred to use).[6]

In 1638, Williams and 11 other settlers organized a Baptist church in Providence—the first of that denomination in America. They had no building, but that was not critical, for the church was the people, the congregation. A building was only a "meetinghouse," never to be equated with the real substance of a church—namely, its members. One did not automatically become a member of the church by moving to Providence, by acquiring land, or by voting or paying taxes. Government pertained to "civil things only." The church was entirely different, wholly separate. One had to take the active and deliberate step of choosing to join the church. One first made a confession of faith, then was baptized, and only after this was the man or woman received into the fellowship or membership of the church. Like the town itself, this church was a story of small beginnings.

Those beginnings seemed seriously threatened, not by an outside force or a Bay Colony enemy, but by Roger Williams himself. Ever restless, Williams kept searching his Bible for evidence of the "true church." What he concluded, after only a few months in this Baptist church, was that the true church must await the return of Christ to the earth. Then Christ could appoint new apostles to take the place of the apostles in the New Testament who had created a pure church. But now the age of the apostles had passed, and not until Christ returned to create new ones could a genuine New Testament church come into being. If, therefore, no true church currently existed, this meant that even the church in Providence did not measure up to the biblical standard. So Williams left the church he had helped to create. But the church endured, as did Williams's own interest in and support for that tiny knot of Baptist believers. He would continue to defend and inspire them in the cause of religious liberty.[7]

Rhode Island itself soon became, if not an inspiration, at least a haven for those seeking refuge from persecution and repression. In Massachusetts Anne Hutchinson, a midwife and theologian, had dared to hold religious gatherings in her own home. Further, she had dared to lead theological discussions there that soon brought her to the attention of the Bay Colony authorities. They listened to many reports about her and did not like what they heard.

All Puritans agreed that salvation was a gift of God. It was God's choice, not man's or woman's, that made salvation possible. One could not earn, could not work for, could not merit salvation. Good works were, as the Bible said, "filthy rags" in the sight of the Lord. Grace—God's free gift of saving love—was all that could redeem someone. Anne Hutchinson was on solid ground in proclaiming all this, steadily and boldly. The ground shifted a bit, however, when she went on to assert that because morality did not bring about salvation, then morality and religion were two separate matters. Just as one did not earn salvation by being moral, so one did not after salvation necessarily demonstrate a higher, more faithful, moral code. What Hutchinson came dangerously close to saying was that religion and morality had absolutely nothing to do with each other.

This idea challenged the foundation of the Puritan social order as seriously as Williams, in his charges about who really owned the land, challenged their political order. The magistrates of Massachusetts decided to warn Hutchinson as Williams had been warned. But Hutchinson, like Williams, paid little heed to warnings. So in November 1637 the General Court, with John Winthrop once more presiding, felt called upon to summon this radical to appear before them. Hutchinson had complained against the Bay Colony's ministers, including her own pastor, because they did not give sufficient emphasis to the all-sufficient power of God's grace. The court pointed out that she had said things "very prejudicial to the honor of the churches and the ministers thereof." She had disturbed the peace of the colony and had persisted in holding private meetings in her home. Such things, said Winthrop, were neither proper "in the sight of God nor fitting for your sex."[8]

When asked by what authority she taught doctrines not supported by the colony's official teachers, Hutchinson replied, perilously, that private revelations had been granted to her. Hutchinson claimed she needed neither the Bible nor the ministry, for the Holy Spirit spoke directly to her. For those charged with maintaining an orderly society, this was terrifying indeed. This way all persons, male or female, could become their own authority, not bound by the counsel of their elders or their betters. The inevitable result would be not harmony but anarchy. This the court could not tolerate. The judgment was clear, as it had been with Roger Williams just two years earlier: "She shall be banished out of our liberties and imprisoned 'til she be sent away."[9]

Banished, but to what place? When Williams had been banished, only wilderness awaited him. But Anne Hutchinson and her many followers had a better option: Rhode Island. With the help of Roger Williams, who interceded with the Indians, the followers of Hutchinson were able to purchase land on the largest island in Narragansett Bay, sometimes called Aquidneck and sometimes simply Rhode Island. In March 1638, some 80 householders, still in Boston, signed a civil compact "solemnly in the presence of Jehovah" to form themselves into "a body politic, & as He shall help will submit our persons, lives, and estates unto our Lord Jesus Christ, the King of Kings." Roger Williams indicated that he had many conversations with Anne Hutchinson, some on religious matters and others on the urgent matter of finding refuge. The town of Portsmouth, on the northern end of Aquidneck Island, became that refuge for Hutchinson and her large following.[10]

With the creation of Portsmouth, Williams's colony was growing. The name of Providence or, later, Providence Plantations, would not be sufficient to cover an ever-growing enterprise. One year after the founding of Portsmouth, at the other end of Aquidneck Island, the town of Newport would appear. The major figure in the first decade or two of Newport's history was another clergy-man, John Clarke. Clarke had left Massachusetts voluntarily, agreeing with Anne Hutchinson that the clergy there gave too much attention to "good works" and not enough to God's grace. In Newport Clarke organized America's second Baptist church. Unlike Williams, Clarke remained a Baptist all his life, even as he remained a stalwart defender of the rights of Rhode Island against the greedy land grabs of neighboring colonies.[11]

Now three towns tried to enter into some governmental harmony: Providence, Portsmouth, and Newport. A fourth, Warwick, would soon join them. That addition was the work of Samuel Gorton, an abrasive and difficult spokesman. But if Williams maintained good relations with Anne Hutchinson and John Clarke, he failed to achieve that level of friendship with Gorton. Gorton had arrived in Massachusetts in 1636, just months after Williams had left. His singular opinions soon made him unwelcome there, so he drifted southward—as Williams had—to the Plymouth Colony. By 1638 he had worn out his welcome there and decided to cast his lot with the Hutchinson group in Portsmouth. But Gorton was a hard man to endure. He questioned all authority, civil or clerical, questioned the existence of heaven and hell, and denied the doctrine of the Trinity (traditionally defined as God the Father, God the Son, and God the Holy Spirit). He was jailed, whipped, and ultimately banished from the island of Aquidneck. That, of course, made Providence his obvious next stop.

Williams did not greet Gorton's arrival in early 1641 with joy. Quite the opposite, as his letter to John Winthrop in March 1641, makes clear: "Master Gorton, having foully abused high and low at Aquidneck, is now bewitching and bemaddening poor Providence."[12] Gorton had attacked all authorities in the most abusive fashion and had attacked the ordinances of the church, baptism, and the Lord's Supper as improper and invalid. Williams, who was generally prepared to accept any dissenter or religious malcontent, drew the line at Gorton. He stood against Gorton's becoming a citizen of the town and against extending any of the privileges of the town to him. Gorton, he said, must first reform "his uncivil and inhumane practices at Portsmouth" before he could be accepted at Providence. If Gorton stayed, Williams strongly hinted that he would leave. But it was Gorton who left, first for England, where he persuaded the Earl of Warwick to defend his claims to a portion of Rhode Island around Shawomet, about ten miles south of Providence. Then, returning to America in 1648, Gorton settled at Shawomet, which he promptly renamed Warwick in honor of his noble protector.[13]

By this latter date, the colony of Rhode Island consisted of four towns: Providence, Portsmouth, Newport, and Warwick. Even more important, Rhode Island had by this time won from England its very own charter. In bringing about this achievement, the central figure, to no one's surprise, was Roger Williams. Recognizing that Rhode Island could have no peace from its neighbors and no domestic tranquility until its legal base was secure, Williams left for London in the summer of 1643. For him the most convenient route would have been to take a ship from Boston because no transatlantic vessels sailed from Providence. But Williams was still under the order of banishment in Massachusetts; to travel there would be to risk arrest that would delay or even cancel his mission. So, less conveniently, he made his way to New Amsterdam (now New York) to deal with the Dutch for his passage. That he knew the Dutch language certainly helped; by March he was aboard a ship bound for London. As the ship eased out of the harbor, Williams saw evidence of the warfare then under way between the Dutch and the Mohawks. "Mine eyes saw their flames at the town's end, and the flights and hurries of men, women, and children."[14] Unhappily, among the victims of the Mohawk attack was Anne Hutchinson who, with some of her children, had by this time moved from Portsmouth to Long Island.

If New Amsterdam was in turmoil, Williams found an England plunged into even greater strife. The forces of Parliament were arrayed against those of King Charles I in a bloody civil war. In June 1643, Parliament abandoned all pretext of loyalty to the king. Before the decade was over, the king was beheaded by order of Parliament, with Oliver Cromwell assuming power as the Great Protector. The middle of a civil war did not seem like a promising time for a tiny settlement 3,000 miles away to be asking for special attention and particular favor. However, many of Williams's old friends, long outside the centers of power, now exercised great influence in Parliament. The Church of England and the king were at this point the outsiders: not calling the shots, not wielding their unchallenged swords, not persecuting or banishing. The worst of times for England might prove to be the best of times for Roger Williams.[15]

And so he proceeded to lobby and persuade on behalf of his poor colony. He established a good relationship with Oliver Cromwell, the two men discussing such theological questions as when the world might come to an end and Christ return to earth. Other friends, such as Sir Henry Vane, shared with Roger Williams the "honor" of having been exiled from Massachusetts because of aligning himself with the party of Anne Hutchinson. But if Vane had lost power and prestige in Massachusetts, he gained both in London and in Parliament. As his fortunes rose, so did those of Williams as far as obtaining a charter for Rhode Island was concerned. Another friend, the poet John Milton, published a treatise calling for freedom of the press at the same time that Williams published his treatise calling for freedom of religion. Milton even recommended his own printer, Gregory Dexter, to Williams for this task. Williams liked Dexter and his work so much that he took him back to Rhode Island with him.[16]

But not before getting that all-important charter. Charters were normally granted by the king or, at the very least, in the name of the king. But now no king sat on the throne. In this unusual circumstance, Williams turned to Parliament itself for his charter. After many months of political maneuvering and pleading, in March 1644 Parliament looked with favor upon the humble petition from Providence Plantations. Williams still had enemies, of course, even in England, but at this juncture he had even more friends. The crucial committee acted favorably, with only two votes to spare. Williams eagerly grasped the document delivered to him: "A Free Charter of Civil Incorporation and Government for the Providence Plantations in the Narragansett Bay in New England."[17]

The name "Rhode Island" does not even appear in this title because the inhabitants of Portsmouth and Newport were still arguing about just what to call their island. But the charter did name those two towns, along with Providence, in the formal legal language of the day: "Whereas divers well-affected and industrious English inhabitants in the towns of Providence, Portsmouth, and Newport . . . have adventured to make a nearer neighborhood . . . and society to and with the great body of the Narragansetts, which may in time, by the blessing of God upon their endeavors, lay a surer foundation of happiness to all America. . . ."

This "whereas," followed by other such stipulations, led to the final and most welcome grant of a charter. The government thus incorporated was "civil": That is, nothing was said about the religious duties and responsibilities of the government, for it had none. Any state that Roger Williams had anything to do with would concern itself with secular, or civil, matters only.[18]

When in 1657 English authorities wrote to the legislators of Rhode Island, asking for their help in stamping out the new sect of Quakers (radical Protestants who arose during Comwell's time), the General Assembly calmly replied: "We have no law among us whereby to punish any for only declaring . . . their minds and understanding concerning the things and ways of God, as to salvation and eternal condition."[19] Just as Williams rejected the notion of a divine right of kings—that kings were empowered by God to rule—so he discarded the idea of a divine origin for government. Government came from the people; it arose from a covenant, a voluntary agreement, as in the first days in Providence. Government was good, a legitimate function of citizens banded together. But government had no special sanctity, and certainly no divinity.

With his precious parchment in hand, in August 1644 Roger Williams set sail for America. This time he could land in Boston because several powerful members of Parliament had given him a letter to the governor of Massachusetts, formally requesting that Williams be granted the right of safe passage from Boston back to the boundaries of Rhode Island. The letter also spoke, with sadness, of the disagreements between the Bay Colony and Williams, reminding all who would listen that they should not be enemies. Their common enemy remained the Church of England and its heavy-handed, persecuting bishops. Massachusetts was not fully persuaded, however, for even as Williams was en route, the General Court passed a harsh law against all Baptists, or "Anabaptists," charging them with being "incendiaries of commonwealths & the infectors of persons in main matters of religion." Anyone opposing infant baptism or persuading others to oppose it, together with anyone resisting the civil magistrate's rule in matters of religion, "shall be sentenced to banishment."[20]

But Massachusetts, under pressure from Parliament, did allow Williams to make his way safely, without arrest or interference, from Boston to his own colony. With those who accompanied him from London, Williams set out on foot on the 40-mile trek to Providence—but this time not through winter snows. As he and his party drew nearer to his home, many prepared to give him a rousing welcome as canoes crowded around to assist him across the Seekonk River. This September was made even more joyful because he could for the first time greet another son, born during his stay in London. The family reunion had only a few weeks for celebration, however, because in November, Williams, now in his early forties, was elected "chief officer" of the newly chartered colony.[21]

The duties of a chief officer ranged from the petty to the substantial. Governing a small colony resembled in many respects the kinds of duties assumed in that period by a town council or even a neighborhood association. One of the problems that Williams faced quite early was wolves: how to control them or get rid of them. On Aquidneck Island, some Narragansett Indians were hired to destroy the wolves, with a bounty to be paid them or any English hunter who brought in "any of the wolves' heads that are upon the Island." In Providence, Williams urged the town to find "some speedy course of [payment] for killing a wolf." New settlers had little hope of building up their flocks of sheep or herds of cattle as long as wolves freely roamed and ferociously attacked.[22]

Then, more humanely, Roger Williams expressed his concern for the needy, the widowed, the orphaned, the unmarried, and the mentally ill in his colony. In a letter to the town fathers (January 22, 1651), Williams urged that a certain Widow Smith be dealt with fairly. Her husband, John, had operated a grist mill (for grinding grain) for the whole town. Now, in his absence, the widow and her son needed some of the product of the mill to survive. How much should belong to the town, and how much to the family? The tensions grew to the point that Williams begged the town to "study how to put an end to that controversy." The deceased John Smith should not haunt them from his grave; rather, Williams said, we have the opportunity to show to all around us "that Providence is not only a wise but a grateful people to the God of mercies, and all his instruments of mercy toward us."[23]

One of the town's leading citizens died in 1647, leaving an unmarried daughter to fend for herself. When Williams learned that the daughter was about to accept a proposal of marriage, with no father to advise or look out for her, he called upon the town for its "fatherly care, counsel, and direction" on behalf of the "poor maid." Williams had some doubts about the reliability and fidelity of the young man in question, which made it all the more urgent for the town to oversee the marriage, if it in fact were to take place; otherwise, "a just reproof and charges [will] befall ourselves."[24]

In a day when no agencies existed to look after the poor or orphaned or widowed, the town had no choice, Williams felt, but to assume the role of protector. Another widow, mentally unstable, or as Williams put it, "a distracted woman," could no longer manage her own affairs. "My request," he wrote the town fathers, "is that you would be pleased to take what is left of hers into your own hand and appoint some to order it for her supply." This again was what a merciful and generous town must do, a town "that hath received many mercies from Heaven." We should also remember, Williams added, that many of us may leave widows or orphans behind ourselves, or be deprived of our reason, and it would be good to have a precedent established for implementing the town's loving care.[25]

Many other practical matters pressed themselves upon the government as well: building bridges, handling lawsuits for injury to animals or property, laying out boundaries for new towns or settling old claims, erecting garrisons or forts for protection against Indian attacks, determining the conditions for voting, and settling numerous disputes among neighbors. Sometimes the disputes became personal. For example, William Coddington, a resident of Portsmouth, had assumed authority over all Aquidneck Island by the time Williams obtained his precious charter. Protective of his own authority and convinced that the "islanders" (in Portsmouth and Newport) had little in common with the "mainlanders" (in Providence and Warwick), Coddington pushed for a division that would recognize his authority alone on Aquidneck.

Williams saw this as a serious threat to the infant colony, a major challenge to its charter, and a personal attack upon himself. In August 1648, he wondered how he might bring water and not "oil or fuel to the flame." Rhode Island, he was convinced, had to take charge of its own house, had to solve its own problems. It could not appeal to Massachusetts or Connecticut to help, for these neighbors would seize the opportunity to divide Rhode Island between them. Nor could it appeal to England, for that would endanger the charter so recently granted. And, worst of all, it could not settle the matter by force, for a resort to "arms and swords is cruel and merciless." Rhode Island's problems, Williams argued, must be settled by Rhode Islanders.[26]

So Williams proposed that ten men be appointed from each of the four towns, creating a grand committee of arbitration "to examine every public difference, grievance, and obstruction of justice, peace, and common safety." Within a month, it was clear that this visionary effort would produce no unanimous results. Coddington, meanwhile, attempted to make an alliance with Plymouth Colony to "adopt" his island, or place it under its civil protection. Williams managed to stop that effort by explaining to his Plymouth friends that Coddington spoke only for himself or, at most, for a pitiful few in Portsmouth. Besides, such an action would violate the 1644 charter.

The charter! Coddington was sick of Williams and his priceless charter. He would go to England himself and get his own charter. Then let Williams or the "mainlanders" do what they could about that. Early in 1649, Coddington did sail for London to carry on his plots and schemes there. By the summer of 1651 he was back in Portsmouth, which was bad enough news all by itself. But the news grew worse: He had in fact received his charter. Appearing before the Council of State in London, he had argued that he was the sole discoverer of Aquidneck Island and its sole owner, having purchased the entire acreage from the Indians. After a year of deliberation and a total failure to contact Roger Williams, the Council granted Coddington his request and appointed him governor for life.

This was a terrible blow to Williams, and potentially to the colony as a whole. Those opposed to Coddington and his unrestrained political ambitions realized that some counterforce was immediately required. And that force had to be felt in London. So, perhaps, two respected leaders could make the case against Coddington: John Clarke from Newport, on behalf of the islanders loyal to Williams, and, of course, Williams himself on behalf of the mainlanders who wanted to keep Rhode Island as one colony, not two. Pressure mounted for the two men to make the difficult voyage to save the troubled land.

But Roger Williams was most reluctant to go. For one thing, it had taken years for the towns to compensate him for the 1643–44 stay in London when he spent much of his time on colony business. Slowly the promised payments began to trickle in, but by 1650—six years after his return—the debt had not yet been fully paid. Further, he now had a large family of four sons, two daughters, and a wife who depended upon him, and he desired above all to protect and provide for them. He was also struggling to reach some kind of financial stability. He still had his Indian trading post south of Providence; he raised goats on a small island in Narragansett Bay; he was contemplating helping Providence to establish an ironworks somewhere in the town. Could he leave all that until he returned from another long trip to London?

On the other hand, no one cared more deeply about preserving Rhode Island's security and independence than he. Also, no one resented more keenly the efforts of William Coddington to divide the colony and cancel its charter. Many settlers, concerned about the security of their own properties, urged him to make this additional sacrifice. In October 1651, he wrote to his Connecticut friend, John Winthrop, Jr., that "my neighbors of Providence and Warwick . . . with importunities have overcome me to endeavor the renewing of their liberties upon the occasion of Mr. Coddington's late grant." Having yielded to their urgent pleas, he sold his trading post and other properties as he prepared to depart from—where? Would it be the more convenient Boston or the more distant New Amsterdam?[27]

Swallowing his pride, Williams sat down to write a polite letter to the General Court of Massachusetts Bay, asking that he be permitted to cross over into their territory for the sole purpose of taking a ship to London. He reminded the authorities that since his banishment (which had caused him "bitter afflictions and miseries, losses, sorrows, and hardships"), he had been a model citizen. He had rendered great service not merely to Rhode Island but to all of New England in peace and in war. "Scarce a week hath passed but some way or other I have been used as instrumental to the peace and spreading of the English plantings in this country." But if any should think that he sought permission to enter Massachusetts in order to cause trouble or create controversy, he "humbly" prayed that he would find only courtesy and civility in the Bay Colony, and he would render the same. He would go directly to his ship, "inoffensively behaving myself." After due deliberation, the General Court decided that Roger Williams could embark from Boston, "provided he carry himself inoffensively according to his promise."[28]

In November 1651, Roger Williams of Providence and John Clarke of Newport sailed for London. These two able, university-educated leaders could move with ease in the higher levels of London's political circles, as they desperately needed to do. Nothing could be accomplished on behalf of Rhode Island without influential friends, without the ability to reach the ears of the members of Parliament who held the fate of the colony in their hands. Williams renewed his contacts with Oliver Cromwell and extended his friendship with John Milton, now appointed secretary of foreign tongues. (Williams helped Milton learn Dutch.) He turned over additional manuscripts to a London printer and shared confidences with Sir Henry Vane regarding affairs back in New England. He wrote encouraging letters back to Providence and after several months in London was able to report one terrific bit of good news. On October 2, 1652, the Council of State had in effect cancelled Coddington's charter and instructed Providence Plantations to assume direction of the whole colony until further notice.[29]

Williams's charter of 1644 had not yet been officially reconfirmed, but Coddington's had been officially set aside. This would do for the time, until the Council gave its "further notice" regarding the charter. How long that would take no one knew. But by the fall of 1652, Williams recognized that such action would not come quickly. The English were distracted by war with Holland, and Parliament was distracted by Cromwell's threats to disband that body. Williams wrote to his friend and printer back in Providence, Gregory Dexter, that "I see now the mind of the Lord to hold me here one year longer." The settling of all affairs and controversies pertaining to Rhode Island will be, said Williams, "a work of time."[30]

But time hung heavy on a man who wrote early in 1653 to the towns of Warwick and Providence, which he represented, "Remember, I am a father and a husband." Earlier, he confessed to Dexter that he had been writing to his wife about the possibility of her and the family joining him in London. "I tell her how joyful I should be of her being here with me until our affairs were ended." But then, "I consider our many children, the danger of the seas, and enemies. . . ." So, Williams concluded, he would leave the decision up to his wife whether to come or stay, "according as she finds her spirit free and cheerful." Mary Williams never found her spirit sufficiently cheerful to make that long, dangerous voyage.[31]

Williams's spirit was not very cheerful, either. He expected to get paid for his services to the colony, especially since that had been the promise upon which he agreed to come. But early in 1653 the citizens of Providence and Warwick wrote apologetically that because of internal "distractions we cannot at present supply you with money as we ought." They would endeavor, however, to look after Williams's large family in his absence. Williams, though grateful to the towns in their concern for his family, longed to return home, but, he wrote, "I have not been willing to withdraw my shoulders from the burden lest it pinch others, and may fall heavily upon all." He would stay at his post.[32]

Yet when he kept hearing more and more about divisions and "distractions" back home, he began to question whether his service in London was as necessary as his service on the "mainland." By March 1654 he resolved to leave, carrying with him a letter from Oliver Cromwell that would instruct the Bay Colony to allow him, once more, to land in Boston and make his way from there to Providence. He did not need to assure the General Court that he would not linger in Massachusetts or cause any trouble there. After more than two years away from his family, the pull from that direction was strong enough to make his march to Providence as straight and as fast as possible. His family needed him, and his colony needed him.

How desperately the colony needed him was demonstrated by the residents' unending bickering and contending with each other. They seemingly did nothing but complain, even against Williams himself. He had had enough. If anyone had a right to complain, he pointed out, he certainly did. Since setting the "first English foot into these wild parts" in 1636, he had done nothing but work tirelessly and selflessly on behalf of Rhode Island. He had done the very same in London. And what had been the fruits of his labors? Nothing but grief and sorrow and bitterness.

"I have been charged with folly for that freedom and liberty which I have always stood for," he wrote. He had been blamed for every land disagreement or dispute, even though he never kept "to myself a foot of land or an inch of voice in any matter." Further, "It has been told me that I have labored for a licentious and contentious people," and Williams was often inclined to agree. One party had even called him a traitor against England, to the degree that, as he said, "I am as good as banished" by his very own people, some of whom said that they wished "I might never have landed" here. Complaints? You want to hear complaints? cried Williams. Then listen. Who was inconveniently drawn away "from my employment and sent so vast a distance from my family, to do your work, of a costly and high nature, for so many days and weeks and months together, and there left to starve or steal, or beg or borrow?" You people, wrote Williams in desperation and despair, have forgotten all that you ever once knew about humility and love.[33]

This was as harsh and bitter a letter as Williams ever wrote to his fellow citizens of Providence. And how did they respond? They elected him president of Providence Plantations. He served in that capacity from 1654 to 1657, when he at last retired from public office, though he never lost his interest in his worrisome colony or its contentious people.

Meanwhile, what about the charter? When Williams left London in 1654, he left John Clarke behind to continue laboring on behalf of both of them to have the old charter reaffirmed or a new one granted. Neither man could have suspected that it would take Clarke nearly another ten years to win a permanent charter for Rhode Island. Amid the many complications that Clarke confronted was England's move to restore its monarchy in 1660. If Rhode Island was to secure a solid foundation on which to build, it needed a royal charter: a charter issued by the king, proclaimed by the king, and guaranteed by the king.

The charter, when it finally came from the hands of King Charles II on July 8, 1663, was everything that Clarke and Williams could have hoped for. It established the boundaries for which Clarke had lobbied, begged, and prayed. It affirmed that the colony of "Rhode Island and Providence Plantations" was indeed one, not to be forever divided between the "islanders" and the "mainlanders." And, to the amazement of many—then and now—it asserted in the clearest voice that "a most flourishing civil state may stand and best be maintained . . . with a full liberty in religious concernments."[34]

A "full liberty" in religion—Roger Williams had been fighting for that for more than 30 years. At this point in 1663, his fight, for the moment, seemed worth it all.

## On Civic Responsibility

*After laboring in London for 12 years to win a royal charter for Rhode Island (1663), John Clarke returned to Newport to put his badly neglected personal affairs back in order. Because he had not been paid for all his years of service to the colony, the General Assembly ordered a special tax on all the towns to compensate him. The town of Warwick refused to pay its share (about 80 English pounds). Much disturbed, Roger Williams wrote a strong letter to Warwick, a portion of which follows.*

Providence, 1 January, 1666

Beloved Friends and Countrymen,

My due respects presented with hearty desires of your present and eternal prosperity when this short life is over. I was resolved to have visited you myself this winter, and to have persuaded you with arguments of trust and love the finishing of the payments relating to His Majesty's royal grant and charter to us. But it pleased God to visit me with old pains and lamenesses, so that sometimes I have not been able to rise, or go, or stand.

I pray your courteous leave, therefore, of saluting you with these few lines, and your favorable attention to them.

On two hinges, my discourse shall turn: first, the fairness and equity of the matter; and, second, the damage and hazard, if not performed.

As to the first, the fairness of the matter. . . . The first is common honesty and common justice in common dealings between man and man. This gives to every man his due: a pennyworth for a penny [spent], and will cry shame upon us that Mr. Clarke should be undone, yea, destroyed and ruined (as to this world) for his so great and so long pains, faithfulness, and diligence. He ought, in common justice, to be faithfully satisfied and honorably rewarded [even if] it had pleased God to have granted him no success, no charter, no favor in the eyes of our sovereign lord, the King.

[Even the Indians], when they send forth a public messenger, they furnish him out, they defray all payments, they gratify him with rewards. And, if he prove lame or sick and not able to return, they visit him and bring him home upon their shoulders (and that many scores of miles) with all care and tenderness. . . . Give me leave, therefore, to maintain my second part of the hinge, which is the hazard we run by not freely discharging [our debt]. We have only three choices. Either Mr. Clarke must patiently lie in the pit, and languish and perish (I speak as to us, for I know there is a Paymaster in the heavens who will not fail him). Or, second, some volunteers must patiently put under their shoulders and bear the common burden which, for myself, I am ready to do, although I part with the clothes from my back. Or, third, the [tax] must be taken by [force] in the King's name and authority, and this, we know, will be more grievous and more [expensive]. . . .

If we wholly neglect this business, what will become of our credit? Will not our stink reach the nostrils of our neighbors, yea, of all inhabitants of the world that hear of us? . . . Again, who knows what storms and tempests [await] us? Who now will ever be employed by such masters, in whatever [difficulties] we may come into? Hath not God taught beasts and bird to be shy of being deceived, especially the second time? . . .

Worthy friends, the changes of the heavens and the earth have been great and sudden, seen and felt by us all this winter. Let us not soothe and sing ourselves to sleep with murderous lullabies. Let us provide for changes and, by timely humiliation, prevent them. For myself, seeing what I see all over New England, I cannot but say with David (Psalm 119), "My flesh trembleth for thee, and I am afraid of thy judgments."

*Four*

---

# A New Dispensation

CHRISTIANS ARE GENERALLY AWARE OF MANY DISTINCTIONS BETWEEN what they call the Old Testament and the New Testament: distinctions in language (Hebrew versus Greek), in time period (from creation and many centuries thereafter versus the first century of the Christian era), and in content (patriarchs, prophets, and kings versus apostles, disciples, and the itinerant ministry of Jesus). But to what degree is the Old Testament as binding on Christians as the New? Or is the New Testament the fulfillment of—or replacement for—the Old?

These questions do not yield easy answers, whether in the twenty-first century or the seventeenth. And some of the irreconcilable differences between Roger Williams and the Puritan majority in New England pertained to conflicting views of the place of the Old Testament in modern Christianity. Williams believed that the ancient moral maxims such as the Ten Commandments were still applicable to Christians in the seventeenth century.

However, the model of ancient Israel as a religious state, a theocracy, in Williams's view, had no relevance to the political patterns of his day. A New Testament, which actually means a new covenant between mankind and God, had clearly and cleanly replaced the Old Testament and the old covenant. A new dispensation had been ushered in, and those who refused to recognize that fact were seen by Williams as following Moses or David instead of Jesus.

Writing at a time when England was delicately poised between stepping boldly toward a full religious liberty and relapsing into the old and tired mold of an officially established Church of England, or perhaps an equally tired model of Scottish Presbyterianism, Williams tried desperately in his *Queries of Highest Consideration* (1644) to give a nudge to history. Or, at this particular moment, a nudge to Parliament, for after the outbreak of England's Civil War in 1642, Parliament was now the ruling authority. And Parliament seemed slow to recognize or accept a sharply new dispensation. In fact, under the prodding of the Westminster Assembly (a gathering of more than a hundred clergymen together with 20 members of the House of Commons and some deputies from Scotland called by Parliament to advise it in this perilous time), Parliament leaned sharply toward the Presbyterian model of church-state relationships: that is, in imitation of Scotland's established church, governed by local gatherings of elders (presbyters) and regionals synods (councils). But was a national Presbyterian Church any better than a national Anglican Church?

At this juncture, Williams acquired a valuable ally: the distinguished poet and political activist John Milton. In Milton's view, Parliament seemed to be moving rapidly away from freedom, not toward it. That august body would censor every book or tract of which it did not approve, and it would move—as all tyranny does—to destroy the freedom of the press. In his most famous prose work, *Areopagitica* (1644), Milton warned that England was headed toward another inquisition. We have already silenced preachers who are not officially approved, he wrote; now, we shall silence readers as well. "It cannot be guessed what is intended by some, but a second tyranny over learning; and will soon put it out of controversy, that Bishops and Presbyters are the same to us, both name and thing."[1]

So the way was paved for Williams to join in the fray. In his *Queries of Highest Consideration*, published in the same turbulent year as the *Areopagitica*, Williams took aim at Parliament's apparent willingness to set itself up as a sort of spiritual supreme court—reminiscent of the action of Henry VIII, who "sate down himself in the Popes Chaire in England as since his Successors have done."[2] Parliament, wrote Williams, knows no new dispensation. "And is this not a reviving of Moses, and the sanctifying of a new Land of Canaan, of which we heare nothing in the Testament of Christ Jesus?"[3] The true church, spouse of Christ, should not be subject to the political "Mutations of this present evil world." England's own history, since Henry, amply revealed the folly of trying to create a state church after the Old Testament pattern. As any reading of the second chapter of I Peter clearly demonstrates, Williams pointed out, the genuine converts to the message of Jesus "as lively stones, are built up a spiritual house, an holy priesthood" with Jesus Christ—not the king or queen or Parliament—as the "chief corner stone" (I Peter 2:5, 6). But what Parliament proposed to do "Mingles Sheep and Goats together, contrary to the spirituall nature of the Lord Jesus, and his true Pattern." This was also contrary to the nature of God and to the peace and safety of mankind. It was impossible for "dead Stones to have Fellowship with the living God," and that must be clear to all of an open mind.[4]

Yes, we have the Law from Moses, Williams conceded, but now we have "Grace and Truth . . . by Jesus Christ." And so as you search the New Testament, please tell us, Williams begged, "where you now find one footstep, Print or Pattern . . . for a National holy Covenant, and so consequently . . . a National Church."[5] In this new dispensation not the slightest hint of a national Church can be located, and since there is no basis for such a church, how much less is there justification for all the persecution and bloodshed in the name of such a church. Even the disciples, when they tried to use force against the wicked, brought this rebuke from Jesus: "You know not what spirit you are of, I came not to destroy Men's Lives, but to save them" (Luke 9:56).

Quoting scripture to make his point, Williams turned to the New Testament, not the Old. He felt that this was where Massachusetts, like England, made its mistake: seeing in Moses rather than in Jesus the true model. Since this point was so vital for Williams, it had to be made over and over, not just in the brief pages of his *Queries*. In his major opus published at the same time, *The Bloudy Tenent of Persecution, for Cause of Conscience. A Conference between Truth and Peace,* Williams produced a work of some 425 pages (as opposed to the mere 35 pages of the *Queries*). And here Williams disputed the sacred character of government under the new dispensation. All governments now receive their power from the people, and ordinary people—the sheep and the goats—have no mandate to govern the Church, "to correct her, to redresse, reforme, establish, etc."[6]

In another large treatise published eight years later, Williams struck the same theme once more. "The Pattern of the National

Church of Israel," he wrote, "was a None-such, unimitable by any Civil State, in any or all of the Nations of the World."[7] The time had now clearly come for Christians to prove themselves disciples of Jesus and not modern versions of the kings of Judah. Here, modern magistrates "have lost the path, and themselves, in persuading themselves to be the parallels" of these earlier rulers. In this great self-deception, "they conceived themselves bound to make their cities, kingdoms, empires new holy lands of Canaan, and themselves governors and Judges in spiritual causes."[8]

Well then, if Israel is not the model for the state or the church, what is? To Williams, the painfully obvious answer was the New Testament, which clearly announced the arrival of a new dispensation. But if that answer was painfully obvious, it was also deceptively so. For many denominations have been created and divided in earnest efforts to respond to the questions: What is a New Testament church? Is instrumental music permitted or not? Are bishops required or not, and if so, what is the nature of their authority? How is the "priesthood of the believer" to be understood, especially with respect to ordination? What is the role of women in the local church? Is the consumption of alcohol forbidden? Dancing? Make-up? Movies? And so the questions continued, in the time of Roger Williams no less than in our own.

The hardest question of all is this: Was the re-creation of a New Testament church even possible in the seventeenth century? Is it in the twenty-first? Roger Williams ultimately answered that question in the negative. Though he participated in the creation of the church in Providence, Rhode Island, he withdrew from its membership after a few months. He did so not because that church had taken any sudden steps of which he disapproved, but only because that church—or any other church—could not faithfully reproduce the circumstances that brought the New Testament church into being.

In the first generation of Christian history, the churches had been led by apostles whose appointment came directly from Jesus. How can later generations possibly match that precise circumstance? Perhaps by an assertion of the doctrine of apostolic succession: that is, the apostles appointed by Jesus have appointed their successors, and those successors have appointed others, and so on down through the ages. This may have been the case through the first 300 or 400 years of Christian history, but then all power and privilege fell into the hands of the pope, the great Antichrist in Williams's view. "Apostolic Succession" turned out, Williams wrote, to be nothing more than "to plead Succession from Rome."[9] Having spent decades in close observation of churches in old England and New, Williams could not find anywhere any evidence that New Testament institutions "are yet restored and extant." Not even Calvin himself ("the greatest Pretender to Church-order") was able to avoid the "great mistakes, and wandrings from the first Patternes and Institutions of Christ Jesus."[10] The sobering fact is that no true or pure New Testament church could be found anywhere in the modern world.

So what is one to do? The answer could not have been very satisfying either to Williams's contemporaries or to later generations: Wait. Wait for the return of Christ, who can appoint apostles once again, reinstitute the sacraments in their purity, and grant an unimpeachable charter to the true church. Based on the Book of Revelation in the New Testament, millennialism, the idea of a thousand years' reign of Christ on earth, was not all that unusual a concept in England in the sixteenth and seventeenth centuries. The defeat of the Spanish Armada in 1588, for example, raised hopes of the return of Christ. Then, two generations later, the turbulence of England's Civil War brought the subject to the fore once again.

In fact, during his second return to England, from 1651 to 1654, Williams spent considerable time discussing the possible return of Christ with "Lord Protector" Oliver Cromwell, who was aggressively Protestant in a way that neither James I nor Charles I had been. For a time, Williams allowed himself to believe that Cromwell's political and military power heralded that grand return. But the restoration of the monarchy in 1660 dashed those hopes. As Williams wrote in graphic language that year to John Winthrop, Jr., " . . . and Yet in the End I fear (as long I have feard and long since told Oliver, to which he much inclined) the bloudie Whore [the Roman Catholic Church] is not yet drunck Enough with the bloud of the saints and Witnesses of Jesus."[11] In less graphic language, Williams believed at this point that the vigorous persecution of Protestants would continue for years to come.

So Williams was not exceptional in his belief in a millennium. What was exceptional, however, were his views of the path that Christ's return would take. Many thought that Christ would return in power and glory, especially power, to rule over a New Jerusalem. Williams did not. Just as Jesus exercised no political power in his first appearance on earth, so he would wield none in his second. What, then, would he do? Exactly what Williams saw as the essential reason for his return: restore the pure and apostolic New Testament church. And that is why one must wait: wait with hopes that rise or fall as one interprets the signs of the times, especially from chapter 11 of the Book of Revelation.[12]

A host of interpreters—and of interpretations—wrestled with such signs as the power of the two faithful witnesses to cause a drought, then to turn rivers into waters of blood, and bring plagues upon the earth; then the beast, ascending from the "bottomless pit," slays the witnesses, who are later revived by the spirit of God, who then "ascended up to heaven in a cloud." Before the monarchy was restored, Williams interpreted those signs to mean that the Second Coming "which I cannot but humbly fear, and almost believe, is near approaching." Why fear? Because, in Williams's words, it will be ushered in and hastened "by the proud security, worldly pomp, fleshly confidence, and bloudy violences of God's own children."[13] Thus, one waits in hope, but also in fear and trembling.

No mean biblical scholar himself (he read Hebrew, Greek, and Latin), Williams found the Bible filled with ambiguities, or what he called "mysteries." And contrasting views of the millennium have divided Christians for centuries. But on one score, Williams could find in the New Testament no ambiguity whatsoever: namely, the total absence of anything resembling a national church, a Parliament that legislated for the church, or an authoritative gathering of clergy such as the Westminster Assembly. Without question, the New Testament was written in a time when the state and the church were as separate as they could possibly be. They were enemies, not partners, eyeing each other with wary suspicion if not active hostility. With only the New Testament as a guide—not history, not tradition, and certainly not the Old Testament—it was much easier to make a case for church-state separation than for any other mode of political accommodation. And Williams would make that case over and over again. He was also vitally concerned, however, to make a case for the nature of that church: pure and apostolic—and wholly dependent upon the return of Jesus for that purity and its apostolic legitimacy.

Meanwhile, one gathered a pastoral church, joining together like-minded believers who rejected the Puritan way of worship that they had formerly practiced and the infant baptism that they had formerly known. This voluntary association was, of course, not the apostolic church that was to come, but Williams did not discourage believers from coming together for mutual comfort and encouragement. And they could, if they so wished, even choose one of their number to function as a minister, to feed the patient and long-suffering flock. But such a minister received no authority from any ecclesiastical official or ordination from any church body. His power, such as it was, came from the people who chose him, and his model for the ministry had only a single source: the New Testament.

The most striking aspect of the original New Testament ministry, compared with that in the seventeenth century, was its poverty. The apostles who had no place to lay their heads depended on the charity of those who heard them. If the apostle Paul was a model, Williams noted, he made his living as a tent-maker, not as a preacher or missionary. "He that make a Trade of Preaching," Williams wrote, "that makes the cure of Souls, and the charge of men's eternall wellfare, a trade, a maintenance, and living ... I am humbly confident to maintaine that the Son of God never sent such a one to be a Labourer in his Vineyard."[14]

The other outstanding mark of the ministry in the first century of the Christian era was its simplicity. With rich sarcasm, Williams spoke of the contemporary church with its "vaunting titles, so strange from the New Testament and Language of Christ." He spoke with ill-concealed contempt of "their holy Gownes (black and red), holy cassocks, holy caps, holy scarfs, holy Rings, yea and holy bootes also."[15] And all the talk of wages, stipends, tithes, salaries, and so forth strikes a false note when compared with Christ's ministers. In the case of the latter, "their owne hands day and night supllied their own and others' Necessities. And this was and will be the onely way of the Labourers of the Son of God."[16]

In earlier times and other lands, priests were paid to pray, or to perform marriages, or conduct funerals. Moreover, "how many thousands are there of instances of moving and removing from Leaner to fatter Benefices . . . just like Servants hired by the yeare (more or lesse) stay not when they hear of proffers of more Ease and better Wages."[17] Clergymen "having been brought up (as we say) to that only Trade" have no other means of support and must make a bargain or contract for their support. Thus, they are "hirelings" who will not move their lips or their tongues unless paid to do so.[18]

Williams left little doubt about what he regarded as a false ministry. But was there any possibility of a true ministry? Yes, but only by a direct call of the Holy Spirit. Had Williams himself received such a call? After he had been ejected from Massachusetts, he received a letter from Governor John Winthrop asking whether his radical Separatist stance had brought him any gain. Not as the world counts gain, Williams readily admitted, but he had won a wonderful prize: "I know I have gained the honour of one of his [Christ Jesus's] poore Witnesses, though in Sackcloth."[19] In a later response to Boston minister John Cotton, Williams suggested to his readers that they should decide for themselves whether he or Cotton most resembled one of the chosen witnesses. Cotton employed force to reach his goals, while Williams used only "the sword of the Spirit, the holy word of God."[20]

Nearly a decade later, Williams continued to explain the place of "Witnesses" in the grand scheme of the Christian ministry. It has become necessary under the "Antichrist apostacy"—that is, the harsh rule of Roman Catholicism—for Christ Jesus to stir up and send out "those fiery witnesses (Rev. 11) to testifie against Antichrist and his several abominations." No ordinary ministry can accomplish this weighty task. Therefore, "Christ Jesus by the secret motion of his own holy Spirit extraordinarily excited, incouraged, and sent them abroad as an Angel or messenger."[21] Were such witnesses university trained, like Williams? Some were, while others will be armed "only with the Scriptures." Yet, Jesus, watching carefully over his chosen, will provide all the necessary gifts to those selected.[22] Without such gifts, a ministry was false. With such gifts, the approval of bishops or kings, church councils or governors, was totally beside the point.

His doctrine of the ministry, Williams acknowledged, was "harsh and deep, yet most true, most sweet."[23] That it was harsh, few would deny. How could a family man, for example, take upon himself the role of a minister that carried with it no compensation, no earthly reward? Is this what a new dispensation demanded?

Once again, the radicalism of Williams pushed him so far ahead of the majority that they lost sight of him—and he of them. You may create a church, he told his readers, but it will not be a true church until Christ comes again. You may call a minister, but if he is faithful to the New Testament pattern, he can accept no salary. Is it any wonder that the number of his followers with respect to the nature of the church and its ministry never became a mighty force?

However, though Williams was still far ahead of the crowd, on another and even more vital subject, the crowd finally caught up. A full and daring religious liberty ultimately became his enduring monument.

## The Liberty of Preaching

*With some cynicism and some sarcasm, Williams described how the national clergy—very nimble-footed—readily shifted with every change of England's political winds in the sixteenth and seventeenth centuries. They did this, he slyly noted, in order to preserve what they called "the liberty of preaching." But, as creatures of the state, as employees of the National Church of England, they in fact had no liberty. Taken from his 1652 attack on such a paid-for clergy,* The Hireling Ministry None of Christs, Or, a Discourse touching the Propagating the Gospel of Christ Jesus.

It is true, I do absolutely deny it (against all comers) to be the Burden of the Civil State to take cognizance of any Spiritual cause; and I do positively assert it to be the proper and alone work of the holy Son and Spirit of God in the hands of his Saints and Prophets to manage Heavenly and Spiritual causes (and that only with Spiritual Weapons . . . ). And therefore the Higher Powers have been constantly deceived by the Mercenary and Hireling Ministry; who being themselves deceived, deceive; and tack about (as the Wind, and Time, and Advantage blows) from Popery to Protestantisme, from Protestantisme to Popery, from Popery to Protestanisme again! From Prelacie [Anglican bishops] to Presbyterie [synods], from Presbyterie . . . many to Independencie [Congregationalism]; and will again [turn] to Presbyterie and Prelacie, if not to Popery (in some cases) rather than lose (as they say) the *Liberty of Preaching*!

*Five*

# THE CHAMPION OF
# RELIGIOUS LIBERTY

WHEN ROGER WILLIAMS ARRIVED IN LONDON IN 1643, HE HAD
three major matters on his mind. First, he was determined to gain
some kind of legal recognition for his colony. Second, he wanted
to find a wider audience for his observations on Native Americans. And third, he desired to make the case, as strongly and as
passionately as possible, on behalf of religious freedom. This was
the driving force for Williams for a half-century or more. That
passion, more than any other single facet of Williams's life, is responsible for the monuments that have been raised in his honor:
from Geneva, Switzerland, to Washington, D.C., to Bristol and
Providence, Rhode Island.[1]

Americans in the twenty-first century may have some difficulty
accepting the idea that one had to fight, valiantly and fearlessly,
for religious liberty. Does not everyone believe in religious liberty? That we can even raise such a question is a tribute to the
labors, three-and-a-half centuries ago, of Roger Williams. For in

the seventeenth century, the answer to such a question would have been an emphatic "No!" Indeed, at that time hardly anyone believed in religious liberty. And not only did they not believe in it, they were horrified by the prospect of it. The common assumption was that if religious liberty prevailed, churches would close, governments would fall, and all moral standards would collapse.

Roger Williams heard those arguments—stated more like self-evident truths, really—over and over. The devil, said Massachusetts Bay historian and Williams contemporary Nathaniel Ward, would like nothing better than to see religious liberty prevail everywhere. A multiplicity of religions would lead to a worldwide loss of faith. Williams spoke often of liberty of conscience. Well, said Ward, let me tell you what true liberty of conscience is. It is the liberty "to contend earnestly for the truth; to preserve unity of spirit, faith, ordinances, to be all like minded, of one accord." For Ward, liberty meant conformity. If pushed further than that, Ward said that Williams and all other fanatics or enthusiasts like him had a perfect liberty: "a free liberty to keep away from us."[2]

Others living in Massachusetts when Williams was banished felt obliged to point out how right the Bay Colony had been to act as it had, how wrong and how dangerous it would be to follow the perilous path that Williams walked. Their condemnation could be theoretical; it could also be personal. William Hubbard, the pastor in Ipswich, observed that all thoughtful persons, both in old England and New, agreed that Williams was conceited and uncharitable. And in the Plymouth Colony, historian Nathaniel Morton declared concerning the "great and lamentable apostacy" of Williams that citizens in general needed to be warned about the dangers of "forsaking the churches of Christ and ordinances of God among them."[3]

For English-speaking Protestants of the 17th century, the most widely read book other than the Bible was John Foxe's *Book of Martyrs,* from which this engraving of an execution is drawn. The book ensured that England's religious persecutions would be burned in the memories and the souls of later generations. *Courtesy of the John Hay Library at Brown University: from the* Book of Martyrs, *by John Foxe*

Almost a century later, Massachusetts was still doing its best to purge the poison of Roger Williams from its system. The Reverend Cotton Mather of Boston, noted theologian and author in 1702 of a religious history of New England, told a story that nicely conveyed his impression of Roger Williams. Mather had heard of a windmill in Holland that in 1654 was whipped by such high winds that the revolving millstones grew too hot and set first the mill on fire, then the whole town. "But I can tell my readers that, about twenty years before this, there was a whole country in

America like to be set on fire by the rapid motion of a windmill in the head of one particular man." The man, of course, was Roger Williams, who had "less light than fire in him." Fortunately, the Bay Colony managed to put out the fire, Mather happily noted, by banishing Williams from its midst. To have allowed him to continue spreading his delusions and fiery opinions would have turned all Massachusetts into a "sink of abominations."[4]

Thus, the seventeenth century did not look kindly upon religious liberty, nor upon those lonely few who advocated it. Williams could talk about it, write letters about it, but could not in New England get anything published about it. The consensus there was that dangerous opinions deserved to be suppressed, not spread all around like wildfire. Williams exchanged letters with John Cotton, his chief adversary in Boston, but most of this correspondence has been lost. Williams would, however, put the essentials of his controversy with Cotton in book form and search in London for a printer who would give his views more permanence.

Before that large book emerged, however, Williams, in London, decided to address Parliament itself. After all, he was on the English scene at a critical juncture, with civil war under way, Parliament forging an alliance with Scotland to help defeat the forces of King Charles I, Oliver Cromwell filling the power vacuum with his leadership and his army, and some members of Parliament trying to find a middle path between the Presbyterianism of Scotland and the bursting forth of new religions that threatened to flood all England. Those searching for a middle way had written a small tract posing the problem as they saw it. As Williams saw it, however, the far greater problem was their reluctance to embrace a full religious liberty.

So he responded with a 20-page tract called *Queries of Highest Consideration*: that is, questions that in those difficult days in

England's history demanded answers, courageous answers. One did not take on Parliament or any of its members lightly, for they held most of the power and had been thrown on the defensive by attacks from many sides. Williams decided to publish his small work anonymously because, he noted, people in power are seldom willing to "hear any other music but what is known to please them." And his answers, if not his questions, would not be all that pleasing.[5]

Parliament had invited an assembly of clergymen from England and Scotland to advise it on religious matters. This Westminster Assembly, consisting of more than one hundred clergy together with civil representatives from Scotland and Parliament's own House of Commons, held the first of its 1,200 meetings in July 1643. Williams first asked what New Testament basis could be found for such a gathering. He had himself searched the scriptures carefully and could find no precedent for this sort of "assembly of divines." Rather, he found only the local churches, only a gathering of the faithful, who exercised no civil power whatsoever. Nor, while he was busy examining his New Testament, did he find anything that looked like a pope or a king who set himself down "in the pope's chair in England" as King Henry VIII and all his successors had done. Religion was local, not national; the church was spiritual, not political, he argued.[6]

But, some might respond, what about the Old Testament? There, surely, one could find spiritual and political power mixed together. Yes, Williams agreed, that was true. But the coming of Christ created a new covenant, a new testament, that displaced the old order found in the nation of Israel. It was time, said Williams, for England to decide whether it wanted to follow Moses or Christ. If it chose to follow Christ, then it could not find in his words or deeds the least "footstep" that would lead to the notion of a national church. If the scriptures so inform us, reason does as well. For reason reveals the absurdity of expecting one faith to fit all, which is as absurd as expecting one shoe size to fit all. As far as creating a national religion was concerned, "it seems not possible," Williams concluded, "to fit it to every conscience."[7]

Of course, Parliament was not trying to fit the religion it chose to every conscience. Rather, it was trying to determine what was best for all England, and then it would simply direct each conscience to conform. But the Bible was full of ambiguities or "mysteries," as Williams called them. How could one hope to solve every uncertainty with such clarity and assurance as to say this was not only true for those of us in Parliament but must now be true for every citizen? We English have been through this, over and over, Williams pointed out. In the time of King Henry VIII, everyone had to cease, immediately, being a Roman Catholic and conform to the newly created Church of England. Otherwise fines, jails, whips, or swords would swiftly follow. Then, in the time of Henry's successor, Edward VI, one had to become a consistent Calvinist or suffer the scourge of the state. Then Mary I came to the throne and demanded that the kingdom become Catholic again, or endure severe penalties. And so it has continued through Elizabeth I, James I, Charles I—and now Parliament. When would this absurdity end?[8]

Thus, Williams put another hard question to the members of Parliament. "We query whether the blood of so many hundred thousand Protestants, mingled with the blood of so many thousand papists" spilled since the Reformation "be not a warning to us." The continent of Europe had now for a hundred years been washed with the blood of people dying for their faith, of consciences subjected to a "spiritual rape." England had up to now followed that same bloody path. Was it not time to bring all this to a merciful halt? Parliament could take that blessed step, if only it would.[9]

Williams concluded his tract with a summary of hard-hitting assertions, so no one could miss the point. First, the ancient nation of Israel was not a pattern for any modern nation, because the shadows of Moses "vanished at the coming of the Lord Jesus." Second, religious persecution was an utter violation of the Christian spirit and of fundamental humanity. Third, to require a national conformity of Jews hinders their possible conversion, because it does not grant them even the privilege of "a civil life." Fourth, religious warfare has been the curse of civilization in that it, more than any other single cause, has been responsible for the murder of countless men, women, and children. Fifth, when persons are forced to conform to a mode of worship that their "hearts embrace not," then they have been violated in the very depths of their being. And finally, anyone who says that he seeks more spiritual light but is still willing to persecute, even while seeking, scorns every standard of both Christianity and humanity.[10]

Parliament was not persuaded. It passed strict rules for the observance of Sunday, with no games or sports, no trade or travel. It required even greater conformity in worship and belief in order to prevent, in its words, a plague of "erroneous opinions, ruinating schisms, and damnable heresies" from infecting all England. Preaching, like printing, would be allowed only under a license from the state. Individual congregations were not at liberty to follow any form of worship they might choose. Considering all this, Williams feared that a Parliamentary tyranny, no more pleasing than a kingly tyranny, would like a dark cloud spread all across his native land.[11]

But he had another land to worry about as well. Beyond the Atlantic Ocean, Williams had confronted a Bay Colony tyranny face to face and in 1635 had lost his battle against it. Now, almost a decade later, he was ready to engage the battle again—not with physical swords or guns, to be sure, but with the spiritual weapons of persuasion and love. With his Bible by his side and his banishment never far from his mind, he would challenge John Cotton of Boston to come out of his study and fight. When Williams had assembled all his spiritual artillery in publishable form, he called it (the seventeenth century believed in long titles) *The Bloudy Tenent of Persecution, for Cause of Conscience . . . A Conference between Truth and Peace . . . in all Tender Affection,* present[ed] to the *High Court of Parliament . . . amongst other Passages of Highest Consideration.*[1U]

Understandably referred to simply as *The Bloudy Tenent,* this long and somewhat disorganized book labored to get at the essence of the argument between Williams and Cotton, between Rhode Island and Massachusetts, between liberty and conformity in matters of religion. Williams called persecution "bloudy" (that is, bloody) in at least two senses: First, its practice managed to spill much blood across many lands; second, as a kind of

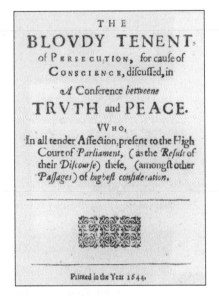

THE

BLOVDY TENENT,

of Persecution, for cause of Conscience, discussed, in

A Conference betweene

TRVTH and PEACE.

WHO,

In all tender Affection, present to the High Court of Parliament, (as the Result of their Discourse) these, (amongst other Passages) of highest consideration.

Printed in the Year 1644.

This is Roger Williams's most famous—or infamous—book, burned in London soon after it was published in 1644 and despised in Massachusetts for decades afterward. *Courtesy of the Rhode Island Historical Society* slang, "bloudy" expressed contempt for and condemnation of whatever followed. A tenent (what modern English calls "tenet") refers to a doctrine or principle that one holds to be true. So a good part of the message of Roger Williams in his 1644 book is contained in the title: The forcing of any person's conscience, against her or his will, is a totally evil deed; moreover, that compulsion was responsible for oceans of innocent blood staining the whole earth.

In all that followed his long title, Williams concentrated on four key issues: whether Massachusetts had dealt with him fairly, whether the Bay Colony churches knew a pure form of worship, whether religious liberty ought to prevail, and how church and state should relate to each other. That was a large order, even for a large book.

First was the banishment, which continued to fester like a sore in Williams's memory. He could understand being ejected from his church if he proposed doctrines with which its members could not agree. But to have his very citizenship taken from him, his right to live and work and feed his family, struck Williams as far more than justice required. He had not been violent, he had not advocated rebellion or revolution, he had not stormed the halls or homes of those in power. Yet, "without mercy and human compassion," he had been driven into the "miseries" of a wintry wilderness, there to perish, so far as anyone in the Bay Colony knew or cared. Clearly, he had been mistreated and abused but now, in 1644, even larger issues were at stake.[13]

Second, how true or pure was the church that Massachusetts had created, and now defended at the point of a sword? Not very pure, not very true, in Williams's strong opinion. In theory, New England made the magistrate supreme in civil affairs, the church supreme in spiritual affairs. There was nothing wrong with that theory, Williams granted. But in practice, the Bay Colony made the magistrate the enforcer of religious duties and doctrines. Here was the absurdity. The governor was at the same time to "sit on the bench, and stand at the bar of Christ Jesus." In effect, the civil magistrate had been made the absolute head of the church as much as Henry VIII or Charles I had been the head of the Church of England. If the colony's officers were the protectors of true doctrine and the punishers of heretics, "what is this in true plain English" but to make them the judges of *all* truth, civil or spiritual?[14]

If the state could compel a person to go to church, why stop there? Compel them also to join in the Lord's Supper, or—even more ridiculous—compel them to be converted. If persons are forced to adopt a particular religion, the end result, said Williams, was that they would in their hearts "be of no religion at all, all their days." In this matter, as in all others, one should take the New Testament as an all-sufficient guide. Consider that when the apostle Paul entered the city of Corinth, he did not go to the city's magistrate to urge him to compel people to listen to what he had to say. Maybe that was because Paul did not fully understand what the New England model of a "true church" really was![15]

This argument led easily to Williams's third point: religious toleration. It should be noted immediately that "toleration" was not the word that Williams would have used, for toleration implied some kind of concession by a ruler or a bishop who had the sacred right to persecute but on some occasions graciously chose not to. This was all wrong, Williams insisted. Liberty in religion was a God-given right that no bishop or king or state or colony could rightfully deny. So Williams argued for, fought for, religious freedom, or as he often said, "soul liberty." This belonged to all human beings by virtue of their humanity—as much as their right to breathe, as much their right as life itself, they had the right in religion to be wholly free.[16]

In his foreword to *The Bloudy Tenent* Williams explained that this liberty must not be restricted to Protestants or even to all Christians. It must be without bounds or limits, protective of all tender consciences everywhere: "paganish, Jewish, Turkish, or anti-christian." Those who proposed religious toleration (as opposed to religious freedom) generally limited that toleration quite strictly. This was true, for example, of England's Act of Toleration, passed a half-century after this book by Williams appeared. That act eased the door open wide enough to include most Protestants, but none who denied the doctrine of the Trinity, nor any who accepted the authority of the pope, and certainly not any who were pagans, Muslims, Jews, or enemies of the Christian religion. No wonder that the notion of toleration held little appeal for Roger Williams.[17]

In his book's preface, addressed to the "Courteous Reader," Williams asked such a reader to consider what Jesus would do were he in London in 1644. Which religion would he endorse? "Mine," everyone confidently replied. All right, said Williams, I do not want to argue about that. But my next question is this: What weapons would he provide to see that the religion which Parliament endorsed was followed by all in England? And the answer to that was clear: none. Just as he employed no weapons in his own ministry except those of persuasion and love, so were only those instruments available to his faithful followers. England had taken steps, Williams happily noted, to see that the Bible was widely available, even "to the poorest English houses," in the language of the people. But how ironic, how tragic, that the kingdom would not then allow people to reach their own religious convictions on the basis of reading their own Bibles. One might as well live in Spain or Rome, Williams noted, where no one pretends that the conscience should be free.[18]

Here in England, he observed, we make church membership (of course, in the Church of England only) a condition for voting, for holding office, for attending the universities. We are asked to trade our religion for political favor, for social standing, for public approval. But this was not the way of the cross, nor should it be our way. "Having bought truth dear," Williams wrote, "we must not sell it cheap, not the least grain of it for the whole world."[19]

That attitude might result in persecution. So be it. That attitude might lead to martydom or death by burning or hanging. So be it. After all, Christ set the example here as well. If one wished only to compromise, to accommodate, to do the nice and polite thing, then onc should look elsewhere for religious allegiance or affiliation—not to Christianity. The sanctuary of the soul should never be invaded by sheriffs or jailers, by judges or soldiers. That sanctuary was, is, and will ever be God's own sacred place, reserved to him alone. Now, in 1644, Parliament must beware that it does not do violence to those sacred consciences. May it never be said "that the Parliament of England hath committed a greater rape, than if they had forced or ravished the bodies of all the women in the world." Because Williams felt strongly about religious liberty and the sanctity of conscience, his language grew strong as well.[20]

To put it simply, the Christian church does not persecute. Therefore, the church that persecutes is not Christian. For religious persecution contradicts "the spirit and mind and practice of the Prince of peace." Beyond that, however, persecution has destroyed and continues to destroy the civil peace of kingdoms, countries, and commonwealths everywhere. Christ is not delighted with the shedding of the blood of others, Williams pointed out, but "shed his own for his bloodiest enemies."[21]

It was now time, if not past time, declared Williams, for the civil sword to be put back into its sheath. If England could do that then it would have a second "Magna Carta of highest liberties," stated Williams, referring to the basic charter of English liberties from the thirteenth century. If England could do that, then every humble cottage in the land, reveling in a new security and new freedom, could decorate its front doors with olive branches, the symbol of peace. Then at long last, the "doleful drums, and shrill sounding trumpets, the roaring murdering canons, the shouts of conquerors, [and] the groans of wounded, dying, slaughtered righteous with the wicked" would be stilled. Here was a voice crying in the wilderness, but a voice that would not be stilled.[22]

Finally, fourth, what of the proper relationship between the church and the state? Beginning with the Roman emperor Constantine in the fourth century, the fatal habit developed of defending spiritual truths with physical force. The emperor Nero, who in the first century burned Rome and burned Christians, proved to be a better friend to true Christianity than was Constantine, for Nero did not corrupt the church by mixing religion and politics together to such an extent that one could not pry them apart. But Constantine introduced a fatal confusion into Christ's religion, said Williams, when he created this political-religious, messy mixture called Christendom. It is because of Christendom that we have come to speak of Christian nations, Christian states, Christian institutions. For Williams, there were no such things. There was only Christianity, a truth that dwells only in the hearts and souls of women and men. It is not found in kingdoms, for kingdoms do not convert, do not receive the grace of God, do not enter into heaven.[23]

So the time had come to undo what Constantine, 1,300 years before, had done. The state had its proper role and the churches theirs. The state might assist the church only in the sense that it maintained peace and order in the society. The church might assist the state only in the sense that it might "cast a blush of civility and morality" upon its citizens. Well, some say, look at Geneva in Switzerland. There, under the leadership of John Calvin, even Protestants had created a solid union of church and state. He had looked at Geneva, Williams replied, and he did not like what he saw. For it implied that the ordinances of the church might "be given by Christ to any civil state, town, or city," and that, said Williams, "I confidently deny." We must not allow ourselves to get hung up on John Calvin, he argued, any more than on Moses. The new Israel is a spiritual community only; the old Israel has passed away, to be replaced not by a nation but by a church. How long will it take for kings and bishops, for governors and magistrates to get this message? They have now had some 1,600 years; that should have been long enough for Christ's words to sink in: "My Kingdom is not of this world."[24]

Of course, Williams admitted, a Christian must obey his ruler in civil matters, but in civil matters only. In religious matters, the Christian may judge his ruler as he would any other person. For example, said Williams, consider the case of a physician who must in general obey his prince. But the prince must obey the physician's prescription for the ruler's health. Magistrates cannot put themselves above other Christians in the practice of their art (that is, religion), just as princes cannot put themselves above physicians in the practice of their art (that is, medicine). This should be perfectly clear, perfectly simple to all, Williams believed. For to act in any other way was "to turn the world upside down." Then the garden of the church became indistinguishable from the weeds of the world. Religion could no longer be separated from politics, and Christ, the good shepherd, could no longer keep the wolves away from his sheep.[25]

Roger Williams had hoped to convince Parliament to embrace religious liberty and the separation of the church from the state. He did not succeed. His book was published in July 1644; in August, Parliament ordered that it be burned. By this time, Williams was aboard a ship bound for America, carrying with him enough copies of *The Bloudy Tenent* to ensure that it would not be forgotten or ignored.

John Cotton, for one, did not ignore it. In 1647 he responded to Williams with his own book: *The Bloudy Tenent, Washed and Made White in the Bloud of the Lamb*. Cotton and Williams had, like two skilled fencers, been dueling for more than ten years. Each knew the moves of the other, the weak points in the armor of the other. Each professed respect for the other person, even though over the years the attacks became harsher and more bitter. Each had his protective shield—whether scripture, or reason, or experience—and would not under any circumstances set it aside.

On the matter of Williams's banishment, Cotton explained that he himself had had no direct role to play in that. Then, in the manner of a parent instructing a difficult and stubborn child, Cotton tried to make clear that Williams had really banished himself. He had refused to be instructed or enlightened, refused to admit his errors and "corrupt doctrines." "You overheated yourself in reasoning and disputing," Cotton explained. You found errors and failings in everyone else, "rather than in yourself." In fact, Cotton added, "I would think it a work of mercy of God to banish me from the civil society of such a commonwealth, when I could not enjoy the holy fellowship of any." Don't blame us, Roger Williams; blame yourself.[26]

Cotton took the purity of the Massachusetts churches so seriously that he wrote extensively on that subject, both in this book and others to come. The Puritans' churches were not really pure, Williams had argued, but Cotton replied that Williams demanded a level of purity beyond the reach of mortal man. We have decried the pollutions of the national church, said Cotton, and we "humble our souls" for having formerly been part of that corrupt establishment. But "we deny that it is necessary to church fellowship" to explicitly condemn and "bewail all the pollutions" of the Church of England. All that was necessary was that members "be ready in preparation of heart, as they shall see more light, so to hate more and more every false way." Williams demanded instant transformation; we, much more realistically, said Cotton, expect a steady pilgrimage from darkness to light.[27]

On the more central matter of religious liberty, Cotton and Williams took a parable from the New Testament and wrested from it every possible ounce of meaning. Of course, they came out on opposite sides. The parable concerned the wheat and the tares (or weeds). A farmer's enemy had deliberately planted weeds in his wheat field. The laborers were ready to rip them out, but the farmer said that would also disturb the growing wheat. So, he advised: "Let both grow together until the harvest; and in the time of harvest, I will say to the reapers, Gather ye together first the tares, and bind them in bundles to burn them, but gather the wheat into my barn" (Matthew 13:24–30). Now, Jesus said that the kingdom of heaven was like this field of wheat and tares, so just what was the message?

For Williams the message was clear: Saints and sinners could live together and even worship together until God at the time of the harvest (the judgment day) made the sure separation of wheat from tares, of saints from sinners.[28] Cotton held that the words were taken out of context and that the historical examples were arbitrarily selected. First, in all the talk about conscience, one must distinguish between a "conscience rightly informed" and an "erroneous and blind conscience." The former must be honored and listened to, but not the latter. Can anyone really believe, Cotton wonderingly asked, that a "heretic, after once or twice" being admonished, "may be tolerated either in the church without excommunication, or in the Commonwealth without such punishment as may preserve others from dangerous and damnable infection?" For Cotton, the question answered itself. Heresy was like a plague or a disease. To tolerate it, or—worse—to grant it liberty, was to invite disaster down upon the entire social order. No reasonable human being would support that. Except, of course, Roger Williams.[29]

Williams also could not believe that the Puritans who had themselves fled from persecution in England would end up persecuting others in Massachusetts. How could John Cotton justify or explain that? Easily, said Cotton. "We believe there is a vast difference between men's inventions and God's institutions. We fled from men's inventions," he explained, but "we compel none to men's inventions." In other words, we and God are in perfect agreement; if you resist our way, you resist God's institutions.[30]

Regarding the matter of separating church and state, again, no reasonable human being, Cotton asserted, would not grant to the magistrate the right to enforce the first four commandments, concerning loving God and not cursing him, forbidding idolatry, and preserving Sunday (or the Sabbath) as a holy day. No reasonable human being could fail to see in the Old Testament the example of a civil order giving its support and protection to the religious order. Except, of course, Roger Williams, who thought that Jesus had replaced Moses and was convinced that Christianity never shined so brightly as when it was persecuted. Just as stars are brightest on the darkest nights and as spices give off their finest aromas when ground, pounded, and burned, so Christianity flourishes not in the arms of kings and princes but when it stands boldly against them—and alone.[31]

These arguments could and did cover the same ground so often that their original paths had been destroyed. These fields of discussion had been plowed from every direction and at varying depths. Williams did not budge Cotton, nor did Cotton dislodge Williams from his dug-in positions. With *The Bloudy Tenent* under his arm and in his heart, Williams returned to Providence.

Back in Rhode Island, Roger Williams did not have to wait long to discover that the controversy between him and Cotton was more than a matter of mere words. Religious liberty could still be denied, blood could still be shed. Down in Newport, John Clarke, along with two other members of his Baptist church, responded to the plea of a blind Baptist in Massachusetts to hold a service of worship in his home. Ever since the 1644 law against Baptists, no Baptist church could legally exist within the borders of the Bay Colony. On July 16, 1651, therefore, the three Newporters journeyed to Lynn, Massachusetts, where they preached, prayed, baptized new believers, and served communion—all in the home of the aged Baptist who had invited them.

On July 20, as John Clarke was expounding the gospel, two constables "with their clamorous tongues" interrupted the meeting and arrested the three "strangers," as Clarke later described the event. After a week or more in a Boston jail, the three were brought into court, tried in the morning, and sentenced in the afternoon, "without," said Clarke, "producing either accuser, witness, jury, law of God or man." They had been charged with "seducing the subjects of this Commonwealth from the truth of the Gospel of Jesus Christ" and with daring to baptize those who, as infants, had been baptized before. Clarke demanded the right to be heard on behalf of the three defendants, but his request was denied. All three were fined, with the stipulation that if the fines were not paid they would be "well whipped."

Eventually, during August friends paid the fines of two of the three. Only one, Obadiah Holmes, did not pay his fine and refused to let others pay it. On September 5 he was brought to Boston's marketplace, tied to a post, and stripped to the waist to receive 30 lashes with a three-pronged whip on his bare back. Holmes responded to his persecutors, saying: "I am now come to be baptized in afflictions by your hands."[32]

When Roger Williams heard of this event, he was enraged. Normally, when he wrote to a governor of Massachusetts, he was respectful and restrained. This time he was neither, as he addressed Governor John Endicott in the severest tones. What possible justification could the governor offer for this barbaric treatment of a fellow Christian? How is it, Williams asked, that persons speak so tenderly of their own consciences yet have "so little respect, mercy, or pity to the like conscientious persuasion of other men?" Oh, please do not tell me that this poor Baptist, Obadiah Holmes, sinned against his own conscience. I have heard all that before, and not only from John Cotton. For "that is the outcry of Pope and Prelates, and Scotch Presbyterians, who would fire all the world, to be avenged on the . . . blasphemous heretics, the seducing heretics" and whoever else dared to provoke them.

Governor Endicott, he wrote, please have respect for conscience, every conscience. Do "remember that that thing which we call conscience is of such a nature (especially in Englishmen) as once a pope in Rome . . . himself observed that although it be groundless, false, and deluded, yet it is not by any arguments or torments easily removed." Besides, how can you be so certain that you are right, and that so many millions of others are wrong? How can you be sure that in persecuting the many you do not end up persecuting Christ himself?

Listen carefully, governor. For you may hear "a dreadful voice from the King of Kings, the Lord of Lords: Endicott, Endicott, why huntest thou me? Why imprisonest thou me? Why so finest, why so bloodily whippest?" The time has come, governor, for you to face a terrifying possibility. "Is it possible . . . that since I hunt, I hunt not the life of my Savior, and the blood of the Lamb of God? I have fought against several sorts of consciences: is it beyond all possibility and hazard that I have not fought against God, that I have not persecuted Jesus in some of them?" What reasonable man, what sincere man, would want to take a chance like that?[33]

The reason Williams felt so strongly about this single event was that he feared that a single drop of blood today could become a rushing river tomorrow. "Like stones once rolling down the alps, like the Indians canoes or English boats loose and adrift, where stop we until infinite mercy stop us?" A fanatical religious zeal, armed with the sword, can be terrifying. God may step in to stop it, but we, armed only with religious liberty, have the power to stop it ourselves.[34]

A former Massachusetts magistrate, then living in England, also condemned the harsh treatment of Obadiah Holmes. He wrote to Boston's church of his sadness when he learned of "your tyranny and persecutions . . . as that you fine, whip, and imprison men for their consciences." This letter aroused John Cotton, now in the last year of his life, to one final response to all this nonsense about liberty of conscience. We tolerate many who dissent "privately and inoffensively," Cotton explained, but we have not carried toleration to the extreme that some in England seem to expect. Besides, accommodations in a Boston jail were probably better than those in a Rhode Island home. As for Obadiah Holmes himself, he had probably not been so well fed or "well clad" in years.[35]

Williams, for his part, never tired of talking about liberty, but he had trouble getting others—even in Rhode Island—to understand exactly what this liberty meant. It did not mean the dodging of all responsibility. It did not mean the abandonment of all moral standards. It did not mean defying or condemning all authority. What, then, did it mean? The Providence fathers needed to know, Rhode Island needed to know, perhaps the world at large needed to know.

In 1655, while he was serving as president of Providence Plantations, Williams wrote a letter to his town in an attempt to articulate just what religious liberty meant. It might help, he thought, to consider the analogy of a ship at sea. The passengers aboard that ship had full liberty to worship as they pleased, or not to worship at all. "Papists, Protestants, Jews, Turks"—whoever—all were free to worship in their own fashion, and none could be compelled to attend anyone else's worship. But on the other hand, the captain of the ship had his own characteristic liberty, too: "to command the ship's course; yea, and also to command that justice, peace, and sobriety be kept and practiced, both among the seamen and all the passengers." This was not tyranny, this was civility. The ship was like a colony or a state and, at the moment, Williams was the captain of his colony. Citizens had to pay taxes, they had to fulfill their obligations to serve in the militia, they had to obey— but in civil matters only. In religion, their liberty was complete.

Why should it be so difficult, Williams asked, to see that liberty did not mean anarchy and that citizens had duties as well as rights? Williams fervently hoped that his earnest communication would be enough to "let in some light, to such as willingly shut not their eyes."[36]

Another kind of misunderstanding has historically haunted the notion of religious liberty: namely, that if one believes in religious liberty, it can only be because one is indifferent to all religion. Some people might indeed believe in religious liberty because, for them, religion matters so little. Roger Williams, on the other hand, believed in religious liberty because religion mattered so much.

In his old age, Williams rowed some 30 miles from Providence to Newport to engage the Quakers in vigorous debate, attempting to show them the error of their ways. See, some commentators say, he did not really believe in religious liberty, because he told the Quakers they were wrong! What a dreadful misunderstanding this is. Yes, Williams told the Quakers they were wrong and for several days debated their religious principles with them. But no, he did not prevent their moving to and thriving in Rhode Island. And he did not allow the hand of the state ever to be raised against them. Nor did he fine, jail, whip, or hang any Quakers, or permit others to do so. Williams, who cared deeply about his own faith and his own conscience, would, with equal passion and devotion, ever care about and protect the conscience of others.[37]

Williams had spent so much time in the defense of religious liberty, in both old and New England, that he had often neglected his own welfare, even including that of his own family. In trying to make a living at his Indian trading post, he frequently invited members of his family in Providence to join him, thinking that the salt breezes and country air would do them good. In 1649, he grew increasingly concerned about the health of his oldest daughter, Mary, who suffered from particularly severe headaches. He tried healing herbs and native plants recommended by the Indians, but her condition grew no better. The troubled father then wrote to his old friend John Winthrop, asking about the best physicians in Boston. But Mary's condition gradually improved enough that she never had to make the trip. She later married and had a family of her own.

When abroad, Williams suffered from the long separations from his family. In 1652, he even thought of bringing his wife and children to London when obtaining a charter for Rhode Island took longer than expected. But the trip was both expensive and dangerous, and the family never joined him there.

The private correspondence of Roger Williams to members of his family has, unfortunately, not survived. One can only guess at the tender affections expressed there. A single, small, personal book remains, however, a kind of love letter to his wife, encouraging her in times of illness or depression. Called *Experiments of Spiritual Life & Health,* this work contains no controversy, only consolation. Williams presented this book to his wife as one would a bouquet on a special occasion: "This handful of flowers made up in a little posy, for thy dear self, and our dear children, to look on and smell on, when I as the grass of the field shall be gone and withered."

When life seemed hard and thoughts grew dark, it was time, Williams wrote, to remember that we are on this earth, "like passengers on a ship," making our way to a heavenly home. If defeated now, we shall be victorious then; if despised and persecuted now, we shall be crowned and treated as royalty then. In short, dear wife, he urged, always remember that after our few short years of labor and suffering here, we shall someday reap a "never-ending harvest of inconceivable joys." Beyond politics and charters, away from bishops and kings, freed from all sorrows and swords, heaven awaited.[38]

Meanwhile, the citizens of Providence continued to quarrel, to dispute, and to disobey. Wearily, an aged Roger Williams wrote to them in 1682 to remind them that government was legitimate and had a proper role to play in their contentious lives. "There is not a man in the world," he told them, "(except robbers, pirates, rebels) but doth submit to government."[39] His friends and neighbors must choose between war and peace. The very next year, Williams chose peace, as his worn and aching body was laid to rest. The exact date of his death, like that of his birth, is unknown. No state funeral was held, no monument built, no eulogies delivered. If in later years monuments were erected, they would largely be as tributes to this champion of religious liberty.

## The Folly and Cruelty of
## Religious Persecution

*In* The Bloudy Tenent of Persecution, for Cause of Conscience ... A Conference between Truth and Peace ... in all Tender Affection, present[e]d to the High Court of Parliament ... amongst other Passages of Highest Consideration *(1644), Roger Williams poured out his fury at the absurdity, the inhumanity, of fining, jailing, whipping, or killing men, women, and children for their religious beliefs. All the sword can do, he pointed out, is create hypocrites and enemies of Christianity; it has never, it can never, produce one sincere Christian. (Or, as Thomas Jefferson later wrote, the only effect of state-enforced religion was to make one half of the world fools, the other half hypocrites.)*

What a most woeful proof hereof have the nations of the earth given in all ages! And to seek no further than our native soil [England], within a few scores of years, how many wonderful changes in religion hath the whole kingdom made, according to the governors thereof: ... Henry VII finds and leaves the kingdom absolutely Popish. Henry VIII casts it into a mold half Popish, half Protestant. Edward VI brings forth an edition all Protestant. Queen Mary, within a few years, defaces Edward's work, and renders the kingdom (after the pattern of her grandfather, Henry VII) all Popish. Mary's short life and religion end together. Elizabeth revives the model of her brother, Edward: all Protestant. . . .

It hath been England's sinful shame to fashion and change her garments and religions with wondrous ease and lightness, as a higher power, a stronger sword, hath prevailed. This follows the ancient pattern of Nebuchadnezzar bowing the whole world in one most solemn uniformity of worship in his golden image (Daniel 3).

What sober man stands not amazed at these Revolutions? And yet, like mother, like daughter; and how zealous are we their off-spring for another impression and better edition of a National Canaan (in imitation of Judah and Josiah) which if attained, who knows how soon succeeding Kings and Parliaments will quite pull down and abrogate?

. . . In all these formings and reformings, a National Church of natural unregenerate men was (like wax) the subject matter of all these forms and changes, whether Popish or Protestant, concerning which National State the time is yet to come when ever the Lord Jesus hath given a word of institution and appointment.

*Six*

# ROGER WILLIAMS
# AND AMERICA

WHEN ROGER WILLIAMS WAS EXILED FROM MASSACHUSETTS IN 1635, John Cotton explained that Williams had not so much been banished as "enlarged" to the whole wild country beyond the Bay Colony's borders. Cotton was speaking with some sarcasm. No one, centuries later, would be more surprised than Cotton to learn that Williams has indeed been "enlarged." His influence has grown, while that of Cotton has diminished. The pleas of the Rhode Island radical for liberty of conscience spoke more for an age that would come than it did to his own time.

Even in the seventeenth century, one could detect small signs of movement from conformity to liberty. The 1663 royal charter of Rhode Island, for example, had spoken of Rhode Islanders having it "much on their hearts (if they be permitted) to hold forth a lively experiment." That experiment was designed to test the proposition that a civil society could actually flourish even with (possibly because of?) a full liberty in "religious concernments."

Roger Williams had earlier looked to Holland as a support for his argument. The Dutch nation had excelled in shipping and trade all over the world; prospering at home, it had also enlarged its possessions abroad. And it had managed to do this while granting more religious toleration than was to be found anywhere else in Europe.

Now the time had come for New World governments to test the proposition, to launch out on their own "lively experiments." Following the lead of Rhode Island, several seemed prepared to do just that. King Charles II had in the 1663 charter laid the firm foundation:

> Our royal will and pleasure is that no person within the said colony, at any time hereafter, shall be in any wise molested, punished, disquieted, or called in question, for difference in opinion in matters of religion, [that] do not actually disturb the civil peace of our said colony; but that all and every person and persons may, from time to time, and at all times hereafter, freely and fully have and enjoy his and their own judgments and consciences in matters of religious concernment.[1]

Under all that formal language, the message came clear: The religious conscience was to be forever free. After 1663, Roger Williams often found it necessary to remind his quarreling neighbors that "Our Charter excels all in New England or the world as to the souls of men."[2]

Others, by their acts of imitation, demonstrated their agreement with Williams. Just one year after Rhode Island received its charter, New Jersey (recently won from the Dutch) adopted a charter that echoed not only the sentiments but even the words of Rhode Island's. No person, the New Jersey document declared, would in any way be "molested, punished, disquieted, or called in question" for any difference in religious opinion or (New Jersey's addition) "practice." Of course, the charter of New Jersey, like that of Rhode Island, tried to make clear, as had Williams so valiantly, that liberty did not mean anarchy, did not mean moral chaos, and did not mean that all authority could be defied.[3]

Just one year later, in 1665, Charles II granted a charter to Carolina (at first not divided into North and South) that said, in words quickly becoming familiar, that no person would in any way be "molested, punished, disquieted, or called in question for any differences in opinion or practice in matters of religious concernments." Roger Williams may not have made much headway in Massachusetts or Connecticut, but elsewhere his once-radical ideas were catching on.[4]

Pennsylvania, launched in the early 1680s, did not need to lean heavily upon the precedent of Rhode Island. Its founder, William Penn, had boldly written in 1670 about *The Great Case of Liberty of Conscience*. A Quaker, Penn had known the cruelty of religious persecution personally, as had many of his fellow Quakers in England and Ireland. When he was given a large grant of land in the New World to start his own colony, he determined that it would, from the beginning, be founded on the principle of religious liberty. No person living "peaceably and quietly under the civil government shall in any case be molested or prejudiced for his or her conscientious persuasion or practice." The "his or her" sounds quite modern, but the Quakers, who emphasized the equality of the sexes, had both male and female preachers from the seventeenth century on.[5]

Back in England, more light gradually dawned. A few years after the death of Roger Williams and the founding of Pennsylvania in 1681, John Locke, a statesman and philosopher, published his first of three *Letters on Toleration* in 1689. Although he used the word "toleration," which Williams did not care for, Locke revealed in the substance of his letter many major agreements with Roger Williams. "I regard it," Locke wrote, "as necessary above all to distinguish between the business of civil government and that of religion."[6] Oh my, what a remarkable development! Williams, were he still alive, would have only wondered if Massachusetts was paying attention.

The civil magistrate, Locke made clear, must concern himself with civil matters only, never with the salvation of souls. "It does not appear," he observed, "that God ever gave any such authority to one man over another as to compel other men to embrace his religion." Like Williams, Locke agreed that the human conscience could not be and must not be forced. "Confiscate a man's goods, imprison or torture his body: such punishments will be in vain." It could only be a matter of regret that Governor John Endicott had also passed to his grave by the time these words were written.[7]

Locke further explained (and in the seventeenth century these explanations had to be given again and again) that civil government dealt only with matters of this world, never with matters of the world to come. The church, on the other hand, was a purely voluntary society. No one was born into it, no one could be compelled to attend it or support it, no outside force could legislate for it. Does one need bishops or kings to form a church? No, Locke replied. One needs only what the New Testament church had: "Where two or three are gathered together in my name, there am I in the midst of them" (Matthew 18:20). It is the presence of Christ that makes a church, not the blessings of bishops or the commands of magistrates.[8]

By the time that Thomas Nast was penning his editorial cartoons in the late 19th century, the separation of church and state had in America become a commonplace idea. Here a figure representing American liberty raises her hand, forbidding various religious groups entry into the realm of the state. *Library of Congress, Washington, D.C.*

But do not rulers have the right, and even the obligation, to punish the heretic and correct errors in doctrine? Again, Locke replied in the negative. For one thing, he said, rulers are not that smart, and are not that richly endowed with spiritual wisdom. "Only the Supreme Judge of all men" has that wisdom, and only to Him should be granted "the chastisement of the erroneous." Fire and sword are "never proper instruments for refuting errors or instructing and converting men's minds." Should any doubt the force of this proposition, then Locke said, as Williams so often had, just look at history. Consider what religious persecutions have done to humankind: "what limitless occasions for discords and wars, how powerful a provocation to rapines, slaughters, and endless hatreds." Where was John Locke back in 1644 when Roger Williams so desperately needed him? Unfortunately for Williams, Locke was only twelve years old at the time.[9]

Locke had enormous influence in America in the eighteenth century, upon the revolutionary generation and then upon the framers of the U.S. Constitution. So Locke, in echoing and often clarifying the sentiments of Roger Williams, became the chief channel of those once unsettling ideas concerning religious liberty. In England, Locke had justified the Glorious Revolution of 1688 ("glorious" because it was bloodless) that deposed King James II from the throne and replaced him with the joint sovereigns William and Mary. If Locke's words could be used to justify a revolution in England in the seventeenth century, then why not use those words to justify a revolution (not altogether bloodless) in America in the eighteenth century?

In Virginia, after the American Revolution was won, many argued about how free religion should be. All agreed that the Church of England should no longer be the official, tax-supported, legally protected religion of the state. But just what did the new religious liberty demand? Patrick Henry and others thought that it would be a good idea to make Christianity itself the official religion of Virginia. There would be toleration, but not yet freedom, in religion. James Madison and others thought Henry's idea was not only a bad one, but beyond that, it betrayed the spirit of what the revolution was all about. To resist the party and program of Patrick Henry, Madison composed what was called *A Memorial and Remonstrance*—that is, a petition and a protest—to be presented to the Virginia Assembly.

In this document, which was designed to gather as many signatures as possible, Madison assembled a wide variety of arguments to make the case against any official religion. Not the Church of England, not the Presbyterians or Methodists or Catholics, not even Christianity itself—the civil government should simply keep its hands off religion. Sounding very much like Roger Williams, James Madison noted that "torrents of blood have been spilt in the old world, by vain attempts of the secular arm to extinguish religious discord, by proscribing [forbidding] all difference in religious opinion." Madison would have the New World follow a different path. "The American theatre has exhibited proofs that equal and complete liberty" was the best remedy for religious strife and intolerant persecution.[10]

Sounding very much like John Locke, Madison also pointed out that civil magistrates are not all that wise in religious matters. All one need do is look "at the contradictory opinions of rulers in all ages." Furthermore, once the magistrate thinks he is smart enough to rule on matters of doctrine, he begins to think that he is powerful enough to "employ religion as an engine of civil policy." Then we have, said Madison, a political tyranny as bad as the one we just threw off by waging war against England. The American Revolution created a nation prepared to offer a refuge "to the persecuted and oppressed of every nation and religion." This is "the lustre of our country" and nothing should be allowed to dim or destroy it.[11]

Patrick Henry's bill went down in defeat in 1785. The next year, Thomas Jefferson's Bill for Establishing Religious Freedom, long debated and delayed, became law in Virginia. The new law provided, in words that expanded on Rhode Island's 1663 charter, "That no man shall be compelled to frequent [attend] or support any religious worship, place, or ministry whatsoever, nor shall be enforced, restrained, molested, or burdened in his body or goods, nor shall otherwise suffer on account of his religious opinions or beliefs."[12] The team of Madison and Jefferson was a powerful one, to be sure, but they could not have won the necessary votes without the strong support of such evangelical bodies as the Baptists, Methodists, Quakers, Mennonites, and Presbyterians. At a critical moment in the young nation's history, the heirs of Roger Williams joined with the heirs of European rationalism, or Enlightenment, to write religious liberty firmly into the legal structure of Virginia.

The victories in Virginia in 1785 and 1786 preceded by only a short time the gathering of a Constitutional Convention in Philadelphia in the summer of 1787. The delegates to that convention saw their task as one of establishing a civil government. And civil government, as Roger Williams had repeatedly declared, should leave religion alone. So the Constitution did in fact leave religion largely alone. Only once did the Constitution address religion directly, and that was simply to say what government could not do. "No religious test," said Article VI, "shall ever be required as a qualification to any office or public trust under the United States." England at this time still administered a religious test for officeholding, as did many of the new states in the Union. But the federal government would not. Nor would it affirm any faith, recognize any church, or declare any religious loyalties. Citizens of the new nation would, like those in Rhode Island a century and a half earlier, pledge their allegiance, but "in civil things only."

In the process of ratifying the Constitution, many expressed their concern that religious liberty was not explicitly guaranteed. Thomas Jefferson was only one of a large number who insisted that this liberty had to be clearly proclaimed; it could not be simply "understood" that, since the Constitution had claimed no power in this area, religion would certainly be free. So vital, so precious, a freedom had to be declared, without ambiguity and without delay. To win the necessary votes for ratification, James Madison had to promise that, if the Constitution were ratified, the first order of business in the first Congress would be the passage of a bill of rights. After much debate and discussion, the first ten amendments, commonly referred to as America's Bill of Rights, were passed on to the people for ratification. By 1791, the people had approved. The very first phrase of the First Amendment addressed religion: "Congress shall make no law respecting an establishment of religion or prohibiting the free exercise thereof."[13]

No one person is the author of the First Amendment. James Madison proposed wording that in the end was not adopted. Many other representatives and senators joined in the deliberations that lasted throughout the entire summer of 1789. The task was to find the precise wording that would embody the sentiment neatly expressed by Daniel Carroll, senator from Maryland. "The rights of conscience are, in their nature," Carroll declared, "of peculiar delicacy, and will little bear the gentlest touch of governmental hand." The religion clauses of the First Amendment represented a valiant attempt to keep that "gentlest touch" from invading the private souls of women and men.[14]

It would be too much to claim that these 16 words made everything perfectly clear for the next two hundred years or more. In fact, the U.S. Supreme Court has spent a great deal of time and thought determining the exact meaning of these words, citing Roger Williams now and then in its opinions. But again, the emphasis was on what a civil government cannot do: It cannot establish a national church (no Church of America to be compared with the Church of England, for example), and it cannot interfere, except in extraordinary circumstances, with the religious liberties—the "free exercise"—of the American people. The First Amendment did not guarantee everything that it might, but from the perspective of Roger Williams the New World had moved mountains between 1635 and 1791.

What that amendment guaranteed immediately, of course, was that some of the uglier aspects of colonial history would not be repeated in the new nation. No more would Quakers be hanged in Boston Common, nor would Jews be expelled from New Amsterdam (New York), or Baptists be whipped, or Catholics fined, or Presbyterians jailed. The heavy hands (as opposed to Carroll's "gentlest touch") of royal governors and civil magistrates would henceforth be restrained, forever forbidden to scar or injure the inner sanctum of the soul.

The long-term effects of the First Amendment proved even more striking. It gave all religious bodies their full freedom: Each church was now on an equal footing with all others, now at liberty to evangelize, to recruit, to spread all across the land. Some denominations tested that liberty very cautiously, as one might test the temperature of the ocean with a toe. Others, however, took that amendment as their very own charter and—especially on the American frontier—made religious liberty lively and real. Baptists and the newly organized Methodists were particularly successful in their efforts, so much so that these two groups quickly outnumbered the older, more established denominations such as the Congregationalists and the Episcopalians.

Earlier, back in Rhode Island, some Baptists and others decided that the colony of Roger Williams needed to have its own college, because Massachusetts had Harvard and Connecticut had Yale. So the College of Rhode Island, later Brown University, was founded in 1764. Like the Constitution, but more than two decades before that document was drafted, Brown's charter provided that "no religious test" would be applied in that academic community. "On the contrary," the charter read, "all the members hereof shall forever enjoy full, free, absolute, and uninterrupted liberty of conscience."[15] Such words could only have warmed the heart of the long-buried Roger Williams. His spirit had not been forgotten. As a nineteenth-century president of Brown, Francis Wayland, observed in 1860: the Pilgrims and Puritans sought religious liberty for themselves; Roger Williams sought it "for humanity." There are some men, Wayland added, "whose monuments are everywhere."[16]

Thirteen years after the chartering of Brown, a Baptist pastor and historian in Massachusetts, Isaac Backus, published the first volume of his major work, *A History of New England, with Particular Reference to the Denomination of Christians Called Baptists* (1777). In it Backus would, among other things, correct Cotton Mather's *1702 Ecclesiastical History of New England,* which mentioned Baptists only to dismiss or disparage them. For Mather, Providence Plantations was an example of an "ungospelized plantation." It contained every imaginable kind of religious dissenter and sectarian noisemaker. Within its borders, said Mather, Rhode Island had "everything in the world but Roman Catholics and real Christians." Backus would also set that record straight.[17]

He would do so, in part, by bringing Roger Williams to the forefront of his history. Backus believed that too many people had forgotten all about Williams and what he had stood for and fought for, even though he had been dead less than a century. Especially in the midst of the American Revolution, it was important to recall what Williams had to say on behalf of liberty—all liberty, civil and religious. Gathering many letters by Williams that might otherwise have been lost, along with other rare documents, Backus reviewed the expulsion of Williams from Boston, the founding of Providence and of its first church, his work with the Indians, the publication of his *Bloudy Tenent*—and more. Backus concluded that he knew of no other individual in that time period "who acted so consistently and steadily upon right principles about government and liberty as Mr. Williams did."[18]

In an effort to be true to that heritage, Isaac Backus also acted consistently and steadily on behalf of liberty. He had to resist Massachusetts, as Williams had done, though by this time the new state neither banished Baptists nor tied them to whipping posts. It did, however, require Baptists to register and apply for a certificate that would excuse them from paying taxes to support the Congregational Church—still the official and established church of Massachusetts. Backus refused to register and refused to pay the church taxes on the grounds that government was for civil affairs only. In 1774 all Boston was angry over the British tax on tea, Backus pointed out, so much so that the Boston Tea Party resulted in the throwing of many casks of tea into Boston Harbor. Fine, said Backus, but you could avoid the tea tax simply by not drinking tea.

In contrast, he said, you—the leaders of Massachusetts—have placed a tax on our conscience, on our "soul liberty." For you require us either to pay your little tax or you threaten to lay a greater one upon us. But "we are determined not to pay either of them," Backus affirmed, "not only upon your principle of not being taxed where we are not represented, but also because we dare not render that homage to any earthly power which I and many of my brethren are fully convinced belongs only to God." Standing as firm as Williams had boldly stood before the General Court in 1635, Backus concluded: "Here, therefore, we claim charter rights, liberty of conscience."[19]

Backus lived to see his fellow Americans victorious in the Revolution against England, but he did not live long enough to see Massachusetts surrender its grip on religion. Not until 1833 were the last cords cut that tied the church to the state in Massachusetts. Up until that time, the state's constitution called "for the support and maintenance of public Protestant teachers of piety, religion, and morality." Taxes continued to be collected for that purpose, and consciences continued to be insulted by the government's demands in an area that "belongs only to God." Connecticut, similarly wedded to a union of church and state, had achieved separation somewhat earlier—in 1818, still nearly three decades after the First Amendment had been drafted. When this Connecticut disestablishment took place, former president Thomas Jefferson in Virginia wrote to former president John Adams in Massachusetts expressing his delight that "this den of priesthood is at length broken up, and that a Protestant popedom is no longer to disgrace American history and character."[20]

Other victories for religious liberty came slowly as well. After the American Revolution, only the New England states (apart from Rhode Island, of course) continued to maintain their official ties with the Congregational Church. But many other states retained language in their constitutions that limited officeholding to Protestants or Christians or those who affirmed "that the holy scriptures of the Old and New Testaments are of divine inspiration, and are the rule of faith and practice" (South Carolina, 1778). The 1796 constitution of the state of Tennessee decreed that "no person who denies the being of God, or a future state of rewards and punishments, shall hold any office in the civil department of this State." Not very "civil," Roger Williams might well have observed. One by one the states dropped these various "religious tests," though not until 1961 did the Supreme Court review a religious test (belief in God) as a requirement for officeholding in Maryland. At that time the court declared that neither a state nor the federal government could constitutionally force a person "to profess a belief or a disbelief in any religion." Religious liberty could tally up another victory.[21]

On the other hand, many Americans in the nineteenth century continued to be distressed about these "victories." They saw them as defeats for the point of view that John Cotton had so vigorously maintained against Roger Williams, and as defeats for the kind of close ties that Massachusetts and Connecticut had maintained between church and state. They also did not approve of the "silences" of the U.S. Constitution with respect to religion.

A National Reform Association, organized in 1864, took as its purpose making the Christian character of national government more explicit. Members of the association thought that the U.S. Constitution should have a clearly religious preamble that would read like this: "Recognizing Almighty God as the source of all authority and power in civil government, and acknowledging the Lord Jesus Christ as the Governor among the nations, His revealed will as the supreme law of the land . . ." This long clause would be followed by the familiar "We the people" preamble. The association failed, however, to gain enough support for its change to be made. The civil government of the United States would remain civil. And the reputation of Roger Williams would continue to increase.[22]

Even in Massachusetts. There, a native son and Harvard-trained historian, George Bancroft, startled his fellow citizens by offering a dramatically different appraisal of Roger Williams than that of a John Cotton or a Cotton Mather. In the first volume (1834) of what would ultimately become a twelve-volume *History of the United States,* Bancroft praised Williams as "the first person in modern Christendom to establish civil government on the doctrine of liberty of conscience, [and] equality of opinion before the law." With respect to Rhode Island, that colony was small in size but large in the "excellency of the principles on which it rested its earliest institutions." Bancroft concluded by calling for the name of Roger Williams to "be preserved in universal history as one who advanced moral and political science, and made himself a benefactor of his race"—the human race.[23]

Bancroft's opinion of Williams may not have been widely shared in the Massachusetts of the 1830s. But a century later, the state of Massachusetts took a remarkable step: It apologized to Roger Williams. The form that this 1936 apology took was a legislative bill that read as follows: "That the sentence of expulsion against Roger Williams by the General Court of Massachusetts Bay Colony in the year sixteen hundred and thirty-five be and hereby is revoked." If Williams had been holding his breath in anticipation of his banishment being erased from history, he would have held that breath for 301 years.

If Massachusetts could be so gracious, no doubt the state of Rhode Island should do something more to honor its founder. So since 1939, atop that steep hill at the bottom of which the first settlers had divided the land and built their homes, a statue of Roger Williams has looked out over his modern city. With considerable fanfare and celebration, the statue was dedicated on a

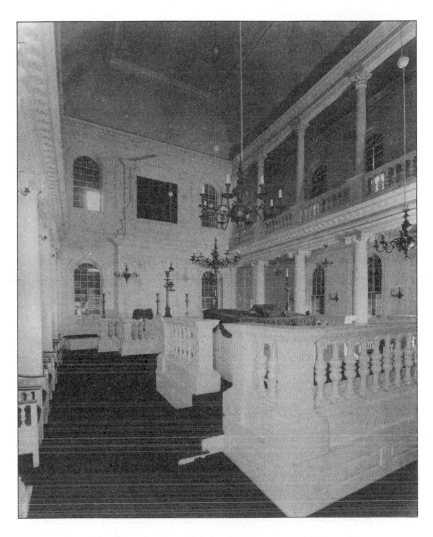

The oldest synagogue in America, Touro Synagogue in Newport, Rhode Island, stands as testimony to the liberty of conscience championed by Roger Williams and by his colony. *The Newport Historical Society*

The oldest Quaker Yearly Meeting in New England, also in Newport, further illustrates the religious pluralism that Roger Williams helped initiate, a pluralism that would eventually spread throughout America. *The Newport Historical Society*

June afternoon with a military band providing the background for a lusty singing of the national anthem. Williams had pleaded for religious liberty for all: Jew, Roman Catholic, Muslim—whomever. It was most appropriate, therefore, that on this occasion the state's Roman Catholic bishop delivered the invocation and the rabbi of Temple Emanu-El offered the benediction. Religious pluralism was not only possible; it could be celebrated, as could the memory of Roger Williams.

At least two other major strides toward "a full liberty in religious concernments" should be noted. For three years, the bishops of the Roman Catholic Church, worldwide, met in Rome in the most significant church council of modern times: Vatican II (1962–65). In the course of the deliberations and the voting on many matters, religious liberty was often mentioned. But disagreements kept postponing a full discussion of the subject until the very end. Then, under the astute, if often despairing, leadership of an American Jesuit, John Courtney Murray, the subject finally held center stage. And the Vatican Council in 1965 passed its "Declaration on Religious Freedom" that moved mountains as dramatically as the First Amendment had.

At this point in human history, the Roman Catholic Church placed itself, officially and firmly, on the side of religious liberty. "This Vatican Synod," the formal document read, "declares that the human person has a right to religious freedom. This freedom means that all men are to be immune from coercion on the part of individuals or of social groups and of any human power." Civil magistrates of the present age, no less than persecuting bishops of an earlier age, must take note. Sometimes called the American document, the Declaration on Religious Freedom gave off subtle fragrances of the language of James Madison, Thomas Jefferson, the Rhode Island charter, and Roger Williams.[24]

In 1978, the U.S. Congress passed the Indian Religious Freedom Act, guaranteeing to Native Americans what all other Americans had been granted nearly two hundred years before. Why was such an act required in the late twentieth century? The answer lay in the many violations of sites, objects, and rituals sacred to the Indian. And so Congress, taking a deep breath, declared "that henceforth it shall be the policy of the United States to protect and preserve for American Indians their inherent right of freedom to believe, express, and exercise the traditional religions of the American Indian, Eskimo, Aleut, and Native Hawaiians, including but not limited to access to sites, use and possession of sacred objects, and the freedom to worship through ceremonial and traditional rites."[25] In 1643, Williams had provided his *Key* to the understanding of the

Narragansett and other native tribes. Now, more than three hundred years later, Congress had found another key.

Being a small state, Rhode Island through most of its history had had no national park. But in 1984, after long lobbying and patient persuading, the state won its first and only such park: the Roger Williams National Memorial. A small parcel of land, just more than four acres and located within a few dozen yards of where Williams built his first shelter, the national memorial was designed to keep the memory and legacy of the state's founder alive. In delivering the main address at the dedication of the memorial, Rhode Island's Senator Claiborne Pell told his audience that in 1636 some 13 families banded together to create "the first genuine democracy— also the first church-divorced and conscience-free community— in modern history." This event in America's history, no less than in Rhode Island's, received commemoration and celebration as bands played and flags flew on that October afternoon.[26]

Roger Williams wrote and spoke a great deal and much of that written and oral record has not survived. Enough has been preserved, however, to fill seven volumes in modern printings. One can distill from those volumes his deep respect for the dignity of every human being, of whatever race, creed, or color. To preserve that dignity, and in particular to protect the spiritual integrity of each person, the essential ingredient is religious liberty. And to preserve the political order, this liberty must be coupled with responsibility. Finally, to maintain any sort of social harmony, Roger Williams also argued for civility. His bequest to America, then, of liberty, responsibility, and civility has enriched the American past and can help to preserve the American future.

## FREEDOM: A CONDITION OF THE SPIRIT

*Harvard's Perry Miller, "the most prominent authority on
the New England mind," also found much to commend in
the life and thought of the founder of Rhode Island, who spent
great time protesting significant portions of that mind.
Miller's book* Roger Williams: His Contribution to the
American Tradition *(1953) concludes with this evaluation.*

For the subsequent history of what became the United
States, Roger Williams possesses one indubitable impor-
tance, that he stands at the beginning of it. Just as some
great experience in the youth of a person is ever afterward a determinant of his personality, so the American
character has inevitably been molded by the fact that in
the first years of colonization there arose this prophet of
religious liberty. Later generations may not always have
understood his thought; they may have imagined that his
premises were something other than the actual ones, but
they could not forget him or deny him. He exerted little
or no direct influence on theorists of the Revolution and
the Constitution . . . yet as a figure and a reputation he
was always there to remind Americans that no other con-
clusion than absolute religious freedom was feasible in
this society. The image of him in conflict with the righteous founders of New England could not be obliterated;
all later righteous men would be tormented by it until
they learned to accept his basic thesis, that virtue gives

them no right to impose on others their own definitions. As a symbol, Williams has become an integral element in the meaning of American democracy, along with Jefferson and Lincoln.

However, the student of Williams's own writings will, I trust, perceive that great as has been his symbolic role, he himself was thinking on a deeper plane than that which simply recognizes religious liberty as a way for men to live peaceably together. He was not a rationalist and a utilitarian who gave up the effort to maintain an orthodoxy because he had no real concern about religious truth, but was the most passionately religious of men. Hence he is an analyst, an explorer into the dark places, of the very nature of freedom. His decision to leave denominations free to worship as they chose came as a consequence of his insight that freedom is a condition of the spirit.

# NOTES

CHAPTER ONE

1. For the Reformation on the Continent, see A. E. McGrath, *Reformation Thought: An Introduction*, 3rd ed. (1999); Steven Ozment, *Protestants: Birth of a Revolution* (1993); and, William R. Estep, *Renaissance and Reformation* (1986).

   For the English Reformation, see Patrick Collinson, *The Religion of Protestants: The Church in English Society, 1580–1680* (1984); D. M. Loades, *John Foxe and the English Reformation* (1997); and, Ethan H. Shagan, *Popular Politics and the English Reformation* (2002).

2. The Plymouth Colony is carefully described in John Seelye, *Memory's Nation: The Place of Plymouth Rock* (1998), and Francis J. Bremer, *John Winthrop: America's Forgotten Founding Father* (2003).

   On American Puritanism, the sources are numerous; they should include Charles L. Cohen, *God's Caress: The Psychology of Puritan Religious Experience* (1986), along with Stephen Foster, *The Long Argument: English Puritanism and the Shaping of New England Culture, 1570–1700* (1991).

3. The best treatment of Williams's English background is Ola E. Winslow, *Master Roger Williams: A Biography* (1957).

4. For the remarkable varieties in American Puritanism, see Philip F. Gura, *A Glimpse of Sion's Glory: Puritan Radicalism in New England, 1620–1660* (1984).

5. John Cotton has recently received major attention in Sargent Bush, Jr., ed., *The Correspondence of John Cotton* (1996).

6. *The Complete Writings of Roger Williams* (1963), 7 vols. (hereafter *Complete Writings*), I:324–325. Also see Glenn W. LaFantasie, ed., *The Correspondence of Roger Williams* (1988), 2 vols. (hereafter, *Correspondence of RW*), I:14–16, 18–19.

7. *Correspondence of RW*, I:19.

8. *Complete Writings*, IV:143–145.

9. *Correspondence of RW*, I:23–27.
10. See Nathaniel E. Shurtleff, ed., *Records of the Governor and Company of Massachusetts Bay in New England* (1853–54), I:160–161.
11. *Correspondence of RW*, II:610.
12. Providence Agreement, 1640; see *Early Records of the Town of Providence* (1892–1951), 21 vols., vol. I.
13. *Complete Writings*, I:298–299.
14. Ibid., I:298.
15. Ibid., I:309.
16. Ibid., I:392.
17. Ibid., I:326–327.
18. Ibid., I:297.
Extract, pp. 22–23: From *Correspondence of RW*, I:65–69.

CHAPTER TWO
1. *Correspondence of RW*, II:752.
2. Ibid., I:54–55.
3. See John Winthrop, *History of New England from 1630 to 1649*, edited by James Savage, 2 vols. (1853), I:228–230; also see *Correspondence of RW*, II:611–612.
4. *Correspondence of RW*, II:612.
5. *A Key into the Language of America* (1643) in *Complete Writings*, I. But this work may be found in a modern edition edited by John J. Teunissen and Evelyn J. Hinz and published by Wayne State University Press in 1973. All page references will be to this 1973 edition. See title page; also, 104.
6. Moses Coit Tyler, *A History of American Literature* ([1879] 1962) I:259.
7. *A Key into the Language of America*, 94.
8. Ibid., 99.
9. Ibid., 100, 101.
10. Ibid., 103–105.
11. Ibid., 107, 108.
12. Ibid., 116.
13. Ibid., 205–206.
14. Ibid., 207.
15. Ibid., 132.
16. Ibid., 142–143.
17. Ibid., 149, 149–150.
18. Ibid., 168–169.

19. Ibid., 204.
20. Ibid., 217–218, 221.
21. Ibid., 190, 191.
22. Ibid., 193.
23. Ibid., 243–244.
24. Ibid., 248.
25. Ibid., 249.
26. *Christenings Make Not Christians* (1645) in *Complete Writings*, VII:36–39.
27. Ibid., VII:37.
28. Ibid. Williams speaks here of awaiting "the Lord's most holy season," as he also did in *A Key into the Language of America*, 84
29. *A Key into the Language of America*, 136–137.
30. For a sensitive treatment of how the English and Indian often talked past each other, see Jill Lapore, *The Name of War: King Philip's War and the Origins of American Identity* (1998).
31. *Correspondence of RW*, II:691.
32. Ibid., II:695.
33. Ibid., II:705, 708.
34. Ibid., II:715.
Extract, pp. 46–47: From *Complete Writings of RW*, III:19–20 (79–80).


CHAPTER THREE

1. *Correspondence of RW*, II:751.
2. Ibid., I:53–54.
3. Ibid.
4. Ibid., II:614.
5. Ibid., I:53, 57.
6. See, for example, the 1645 Massachusetts law against "Anabaptists" in Nathaniel B. Shurtleff, ed., *Records of the Governor and Company of the Massachusetts Bay in New England* (1853–54), II:85.
7. See *Christenings Make Not Christians* in *Complete Writings*, VII:31–41, where Williams expresses his views that the true church must await the return of Jesus.
8. On the antinomian controversy in general and Anne Hutchinson in particular, see David D. Hall, ed., *The Antinomian Controversy, 1636–1638: A Documentary History*, 2d ed. (1990), 349–388.
9. Ibid. Also, *Correspondence of RW*, I:149–150, 151–152, n. 8.

10. Hall, *The Antinomian Controversy*, as well as Eva LaPlante, *American Jezebel: The Uncommon Life of Anne Hutchinson, The Woman Who Defied the Puritans* (2003).

11. See Sydney V. James, *John Clarke and His Legacies: Religion and Law in Colonial Rhode Island 1638–1750* (1999).

12. *Correspondence of RW*, I:215.

13. Ibid., I:214.

14. Ibid., II:410.

15. Ibid., I:288, 291, 317, 358–359.

16. Ibid., I:385–386, II:395–398.

17. Ibid., I:232, n. 4; 371–372.

18. See Edmund S. Morgan, *Roger Williams: The Church and the State* (1967), 130–142.

19. Rufus Jones, *Quakers in the American Colonies* ([1911] 1966), 54–56.

20. See this chapter, note 6 above. Also see Ola E. Winslow, *Master Roger Williams: A Biography* (1957), 176–188.

21. *Correspondence of RW*, I:274.

22. Ibid., I:146; 148, n.9; II:442; 443, n. 6.

23. Ibid., I:329–330.

24. Ibid.

25. Ibid.

26. Ibid., I:167.

27. Ibid., I:351.

28. Ibid., I:353–354.

29. Ibid., I:366–367; 370, n. 12.

30. Ibid., I:367.

31. Ibid.

32. Ibid., I:380–382.

33. Ibid., 399–402.

34. John Russell Bartlett, ed., *Records of the Colony of Rhode Island* (1856–1865), 10 vols., II:3–21.

Extract, pp. 71–73: From *Correspondence of RW*, II:534–540.

CHAPTER FOUR

1. Quoted in the introduction to *Queries of Highest Consideration* in *Complete Writings*, II:9.

2. Ibid., II:19.

3. Ibid., II:19–20.

4. Ibid., II:22.

5. Ibid., II:24.
6. Ibid., III (entire). However, a new edition of *The Bloudy Tenent* is now available: Richard Groves, ed., and published by Mercer University Press in 2001. All page references are to this edition; 155.
7. *Complete Writings*, IV:29.
8. *Bloudy Tenent*, 228.
9. *A Hireling Ministry None of Christs* (1652) in *Complete Writings*, VII:162.
10. Ibid., 160, 161.
11. *Correspondence of RW*, II:500.
12. W. Clark Gilpin, *The Millenarian Piety of Roger Williams* (1979), esp. 89, 141-142, 145.
13. *The Bloudy Tenent Yet More Bloudy* (1652) in *Complete Writings*, IV:26.
14. *Hireling Ministry* in *Complete Writings*, VII:164.
15. Ibid., VII:170.
16. Ibid., VII:165.
17. Ibid., VII:164.
18. Ibid.
19. *Correspondence of RW*, I:66.
20. *Mr. Cotton's Letter, Lately Printed, Examined and Answered* (1644) in *Complete Writings*, I:340.
21. *Complete Writings*, IV:191-192.
22. *The Fourth Paper Presented by Major Butler* (1652) in *Complete Writings*, VII:131.
23. *Bloudy Tenent*, 182.
Extract, p. 85: From *Complete Writings of RW*, VII:152-153.

CHAPTER FIVE
1. Monuments in Bristol include not only a statue but a university that bears his name.
2. Nathaniel Ward, *The Simple Cobbler of Aggawan in America* ([1647] 1713), 6-7, 11. This and all other colonial items are listed in Charles Evans, *American Bibliography* (1903ff., 1941). Said items are now on microfiche, available in research and most major university libraries.
3. William Hubbard, *A General History of New England* (1682), 204; and Nathaniel Morton, *New England's Memorial* (1669), 102-103.
4. Cotton Mather, *Ecclesiastical History of New England* (1702), II:520-521.
5. Roger Williams, *Queries of Highest Consideration* (1644), in *Complete Writings*, II:13.

6. Ibid., II:17–19.
7. Ibid., II:26.
8. Ibid., II:20.
9. Ibid.
10. Ibid., II:24–33.
11. See Morgan, *Roger Williams: The Church and the State*, 99–101.
12. *The Bloudy Tenent.*
13. *Mr. Cotton's Letter Lately Printed, Examined and Answered* in *Complete Writings*, I:313, 396. Though not published until 1644 when a trip to London made it possible, Williams's view on this matter was well fixed by 1636. See 31, 35, 42–43 for references to the banishment, an event that continued to rankle for the rest of his life. See his letter written in 1670 to John Mason and Thomas Prence in *Correspondence of RW*, II:609–620.
14. *The Bloudy Tenent*, 217.
15. *The Bloudy Tenent Yet More Bloudy* in *Complete Writings*, IV:273–274.
16. *The Bloudy Tenent*, 3–4, 31–32.
17. Ibid., 3.
18. Ibid., 8–9.
19. Ibid., 9.
20. Ibid.
21. Ibid., 86, 117–118.
22. Ibid., 134–135.
23. Ibid., 112.
24. Ibid., 91–93, 138.
25. Ibid., 235.
26. *Letter of John Cotton* . . . (1643) in *Complete Writings*, I:14–15.
27. Ibid., 24–25.
28. *The Bloudy Tenent*, 55–56.
29. Ibid., 20–21, 130.
30. John Cotton, *A Reply to Mr. Williams* . . . (1647) in *Complete Writings*, II:61. Here Cotton attacked Williams personally, writing of his "selfe-conceited, and unquiet, and unlamblike frame of his Spirit"; also of the "unmoveable stiffnesses, and headinesse of his Spirit" (14); and, finally, of "the rocky flintinesse of his selfe-confidence" (52).
31. *The Bloudy Tenent*, 112.
32. For this whole episode, see Edwin S. Gaustad, *Baptist Piety: The Last Will and Testimony of Obadiah Holmes* ([1978, 1994], 2005).
33. *Correspondence of RW*, I:347–346.
34. Ibid.

35. The remarks of Richard Saltonstall are preserved in Thomas Hutchinson, *Collection of Original Papers Relative to the History of the Colony of Massacusetts Bay* (1769). For Cotton's unforgiving observations, see his *The Bloudy Tenent Washed, and made white in the bloud of the Lambe* (1647), 29.

36. *Correspondence of RW*, II:423–424.

37. The founder of the Quakers was George Fox, and the movement's chief spokesman in New England (and in the debate with Williams) was Edward Burroughs. So when Williams published his side of the debate, he could not resist the bad pun, *George Fox Digg'd out of his Burrowes* (1676) in *Complete Writings*, V.

38. Here Williams may be seen in his more tender moments, in *Complete Writings*, VII:56, 59, 89, 103–104.

39. *Correspondence of RW*, II:774–776.

Extract, pp. 110–111: From *Complete Writings of RW*, III:136–137.

CHAPTER SIX

1. For the full text of the 1663 charter, see John Russell Bartlett, ed., *Records of the Colony of Rhode Island*, II:3–21.

2. *Correspondence of RW*, II:775.

3. See Francis Newton Thorpe, *The Federal and State Constitutions, Colonial Charters, and Other Organic Laws of the States, Territories, and Colonies*, 7 vols. (Washington, D.C., 1909), V:2537.

4. Ibid., V:2771.

5. Ibid., V:3063.

6. David Wootton, *John Locke: Political Writings* (1993), 393; also, 433.

7. Ibid., 395.

8. Ibid., 396–397.

9. Ibid., 395–396.

10. *The Papers of James Madison* (1973), VIII:298–304.

11. Ibid.

12. For the bill as Jefferson originally wrote it, see *The Papers of Thomas Jefferson* (1950), II:545–547.

13. For the several drafts of the First Amendment before it reached its final form, see Appendix A in Edwin S. Gaustad, *Faith of the Founders: Religion and the New Nation* ([1987] 2004).

14. Ibid.

15. The full charter for Brown University may be found in Reuben A. Guild, *The Early History of Brown University* (1897).

16. Wayland as quoted in a New York newspaper, *The World*, June 16, 1860.
17. Cotton Mather, *Ecclesiastical History of New England* (1702), II:520–521.
18. See Backus's *History* ([1777] 1969), I:75–76.
19. Alvah Hovey, *A Memoir of the Life and Times of Isaac Backus* (1859), 220f.; also see the superb biography by William G. McLoughlin, *Isaac Backus and the American Pietistic Tradition* (1967).
20. Lester J. Cappon, ed., *The Adams–Jefferson Letters* (1959), II:512; the letter is dated May 5, 1817.
21. See Appendix A in Edwin S. Gaustad, *Faith of the Founders*.
22. For an illuminating discussion of the National Reform Association, see Morton Borden, *Jews, Turks, and Infidels* (1984).
23. George Bancroft, *History of the United States . . .* 10th ed. (1842), 2 vols., II:354–396.
24. *Declaration on Religious Liberty*, dated Dec. 7, 1965, and issued by the National Catholic Welfare Conference.
25. *U.S. Statutes at Large* (1980), 469.
26. Program of Dedication, Roger Williams National Memorial; see the National Memorial for a copy.

Extract, pp. 131–132: From *Roger Williams: His Contribution to the American Tradition*, ed. Perry Miller (Indianapolis: Bobbs-Merrill, 1953), 254–255.

# FURTHER READING

THE WRITINGS OF ROGER WILLIAMS
Williams, Roger. *The Bloudy Tenent of Persecution*. Edited by Richard Groves. Macon, Ga.: Mercer University Press, 2001. A readable and accessible edition of Williams's most famous treatise.

———. *The Complete Writings of Roger Williams*. 7 vols. New York: Russell & Russell, 1963. Six of these volumes were originally published between 1866 and 1874. The seventh, containing new discoveries and valuable introductions, was added in 1963.

———. *The Correspondence of Roger Williams*. Edited by Glenn W. LaFantasie. 2 vols. Hanover, N.H.: University Press of New England, 1988. A marvelously thorough and helpful edition of Williams's letters, with extensive notes, useful maps, and an excellent index.

———. *Experiments of Spiritual Life and Health*. Edited by Winthrop S. Hudson. Philadelphia: Westminster Press, 1951. This small booklet, written by Williams for the spiritual and physical health of his wife, is expertly introduced and edited.

———. *A Key into the Language of America*. Edited by John J. Teunissen and Evelyn J. Hinz. Detroit: Wayne State University Press, 1973. This, Williams's first published book, was popular in London in the seventeenth century and has remained popular in America. This modern edition further enhances that popularity and extends the book's availability.

———. *Roger Williams: His Contribution to the American Tradition*. Edited by Perry Miller. Indianapolis: Bobbs-Merrill, 1953. This small anthology did much to rescue the reputation of Roger Williams in modern America, as well as to present limited excerpts of his writings in an attractive form.

WRITINGS ABOUT WILLIAMS AND HIS CONTEMPORARIES
Bremer, Francis J. *John Winthrop: America's Forgotten Founding Father*. New York: Oxford University Press, 2003. Not really "forgotten" (see Edmund S.

Morgan's excellent and best-selling biography published in 1958), Winthrop is here presented in impressive detail for a new generation.

Bush, Sargent, Jr., ed. *The Correspondence of John Cotton.* Chapel Hill: University of North Carolina Press, 2001. Gathering scattered and often fugitive materials from Britain, Holland, and America, Bush presents a first-rate edition of the less formal products from the quill of John Cotton—Williams's leading antagonist in seventeenth–century New England.

Gaustad, Edwin S. *Proclaim Liberty Throughout All the Land: A History of Church and State in America.* New York: Oxford University Press, 2003. A history of the development, and detours, of religious liberty in America.

Hall, Timothy L. *Separating Church and State: Roger Williams and Religious Liberty.* Urbana: University of Illinois Press, 1998. A professor at the University of Mississippi Law School carefully interprets the legal impact and enduring significance of Roger Williams.

James, Sydney V. *John Clarke and His Legacies: Religion and Law in Colonial Rhode Island.* Edited by Theodore Dwight Bozeman. University Park: Pennsylvania State University Press, 1999. The first full-length treatment of John Clarke written by a skilled historian; gives major attention to the Newport pastor's theology as well as his lasting achievements in politics and philanthropy.

McLoughlin, William G. *New England Dissent: The Baptists and the Separation of Church and State.* 2 vols. Cambridge: Harvard University Press, 1971. Comprehensive in a way that no previous work on this topic had ever been, these two volumes place Roger Williams, John Clarke, Isaac Backus, and others in their proper historical and denominational context.

Miller, William Lee. *The First Liberty: Religion and the American Republic.* New York: Knopf, 1986. Written primarily to celebrate the two-hundredth anniversary of Thomas Jefferson's Statute for Establishing Religious Freedom in Virginia (1786), this study gives ample attention to the earlier labors of Roger Williams.

Morgan, Edmund S. *The Puritan Dilemma: The Story of John Winthrop.* Boston: Little, Brown, 1958. This popular biography, as readable as it is reliable, gives Williams's sometime friend and sometime critic the careful examination that he deserves.

———. *Roger Williams: The Church and the State.* New York: Harcourt, Brace, 1967. Yale's Professor Morgan manages to be sympathetic not only to the Puritans but also to their most tenacious critic, Roger Williams.

Noonan, John T., Jr. *The Lustre of Our Country: The American Experience of Religious Freedom.* Berkeley: University of California Press, 1998. Taking his title from James Madison, Judge Noonan (Federal Court of Appeals,

Ninth Circuit) also takes his inspiration from the Madisonian stance. This is a very sophisticated and suggestive treatment of the development of religious freedom in America.

Winslow, Ola E. *Master Roger Williams: A Biography.* New York: Macmillan, 1957. An excellent biography that gives more attention to Williams's London years than does any other book.

Ziff, Larzer, ed. *John Cotton on the Churches of New England.* Cambridge: Harvard University Press, 1968. "The greatest preacher in the first decades of New England history," Cotton was also Roger Williams's greatest antagonist; here he is permitted to speak for himself, without Williams's constant interruption.

# INDEX